This is normally where you w
dorsements from flashy celebri
my third book where I asked my readers to read the book
and share their feedback with the masses, and I loved it so
much I wanted to do it again with this book. Especially since
Turn Toward the Sun is so deeply personal and close to my
heart. I have readers who are also close to my heart who have
been with me on this journey called life for over a decade,
so I honestly can't imagine a better group of people to read
and essentially review this book for you.

So, for you there—yes you, holding this book in your
hands, wondering if you should buy it—here's what real
women and men just like you had to say about it:

"Mandy Hale never misses a (heart)beat! Her latest lessons
in *Turn Toward the Sun* bring essential clarity to love and life
among the post-2020 confusion. No platitudes, just perspective, perseverance, purpose, and peace. Mandy faces life's
hurts and challenges head-on—possibly her bravest move
yet. And the gift to her readers is knowing we can do it too."

Tiffany Griffith, Atlanta journalist by day; hopeless
romantic by night; lover of live music, cupcakes,
and Gator football in the in-between times

"*Turn Toward the Sun* is a down-to-earth guidebook for
shifting your perspective to the light, no matter how hard
life hits you. Like getting together with a best friend who
really sees me and accepts me right where I'm at, this book

made me laugh, cry, and hope again. It's sure to become your favorite quotable inspiration."

Cindy (Goyette) Cook, Nashville single mom, grandmother, wellness coach, motivator, and former break dancer; #SeeYouAtTheFinishLine

"If you've read any of Mandy Hale's books, you know she has a gift for putting things in a way that makes her readers feel not only seen but also in good company. In her latest release, *Turn Toward the Sun*, she does that and more, sharing a mixture of personal stories and biblical references that made me as a reader exclaim, 'Yes! All of THIS!' several times while reading it."

Jenae Ivy, a girl in Maryland, believing the best is still yet to come

"Raw. Real. Encouraging. In *Turn Toward the Sun*, Mandy paints a refreshing picture of a renewed perspective. After 2020 and the Covid-19 pandemic, this book is a true breath of fresh air. It challenges me to be present and own every moment while enjoying every part of *right now*. Mandy's message strengthens my faith and reinforces my perspective in who God has called me to be."

Chris Osmore, creative professional in Kerrville, Texas

"I have read every book Mandy Hale has written—some more than once—and I've loved every single one. But this one spoke to my soul in a way no book ever has before. Much like sitting in my church listening to my pastor do a Sunday morning sermon, every word I read felt like it was directed solely at me. To be able to live in the *what is* and not in the *what if* is something I hope I can put into practice in the coming year. Mandy's transparency and honesty are not only inspiring; they're *authentic*. Somehow each book she writes tops the last one, but this one blew me away!"

Danielle Jenkins, (almost) forty-one and embracing the present one day at a time in speck-on-the-map Pine Prairie, Louisiana

"I've been reading/following Mandy Hale for almost ten years now, and her books consistently speak to me. Her words are balm for the soul. In particular, with *Turn Toward the Sun*, if you're struggling with the *what if* versus the *what is* of life, I encourage you to grab a hot cup of cocoa and settle in on the couch for a comforting read. Mandy's words will bring you peace of mind, which we all need more of these days."

Alisen James, forty-five and embracing *what is* in San Diego, California

"Through her courageous and brilliant illumination of her pitfalls in past relationships, her struggles with adjustments to life in quarantine, and the heartache of personal and family tragedy, Mandy Hale adroitly provides her readership with wisdom and warning mixed with clarity and compassion: a winning combination by any standard!"

Ravi Meibalane, physician in Nashville, Tennessee

"Authentic. Transparent. Forthcoming. These are just a few words to describe Mandy Hale, as evidenced in all her books, especially *Turn Toward the Sun*. Reading this book felt like sitting across the table from a friend sharing stories. Mandy has helped me feel not so alone as a fifty-two-year-old single woman. Mandy's books consistently leave me encouraged!"

"Mandy Hale, one of my best friends in my head, hooks you with the introduction alone. In *Turn Toward the Sun*, Mandy is right on time for me like she always is. In this stage of my life, I am constantly battling between *what if* and *what is*, and Mandy made me realize I'm not alone in this battle. From her words about faith and God to her words about control and letting go, this book made me feel seen. If you are in that 'lost' stage in your life, look no further than Mandy's new book to help you, encourage you, and most importantly—uplift you."

"This book spoke directly to my heart and reminded me that I must stop dwelling in the *what if*s of life and start living in the *what is*. Mandy once again gets real and honest and shares intimate details of her life with her readers. From the effects of the pandemic on her own mental health to how her family dealt with both of her parents struggling with cancer at the same time; from saying a final goodbye to and letting go of a man she, at one time, thought was her future to how she continues to grow closer to God each and every day; along with some lighthearted, insightful analyses of the mysterious male species that every single woman ponders from time to time—this book has something every reader can relate to. I have read each of Mandy's books multiple times (if you haven't done this yourself, what are you waiting for?), and this book clearly demonstrates how Mandy has grown and learned from life's lessons along the way."

Susan Mackey, corporate accountant, single mom of two teenage girls, and child of God, who has been reminded by her favorite author, Mandy Hale, in her books that "my imperfect self is perfectly ENOUGH"

"Another book blessing from my proverbial virtual big sister! To think that reading Mandy's first book eight years ago would lead to life lessons, amazing friendships, and even me helping endorse this book! Thank you, Mandy, for sharing parts of your heart and your life that ended up helping me find and embrace myself!"

Jazmine Thomas, a single woman from Ohio who thrives at saving lives

"*Turn Toward the Sun* is a true testament about being a single woman in your forties: from navigating life in the midst of a pandemic to dealing with cancer, anxiety, friendships, dating, and more. Mandy Hale is insightful, passionate, and completely honest when it comes to describing life as a single woman. Her struggles are our struggles, and her faith is inspiring! This book was like reading my own diary!"

Ronda Darnell, Nashville believer

"Mandy Hale tackles the *real* in *Turn Toward the Sun*. She is bold enough to get downright honest about the impact that the Covid-19 pandemic had on her family, her worldviews, and even her own self-confidence and mental health. She dives into her inner soul with this transparent project. This book will take you on a journey that will help you learn about yourself and who you truly are. This is a bold venture for Mandy and a *must-read*."

Brandon McCullen, writer from Tennessee

"Mandy has always walked a faithful path, in or out of stilettos. In her latest book, *Turn Toward the Sun*, her faithfulness isn't weakened; it's fortified. Here she shines by just being herself, living the *what is* as authentically as she does while knowing there's a light she can trust and always turn toward."

Andrea Mendoza, modestly published writer, vaingloriously joyful mama

"Thanks to all of Mandy's books, I have always felt seen and heard and, most importantly, not alone in this funny thing called life. In *Turn Toward the Sun*, Mandy is real and raw about her experiences through the pandemic and other moments of darkness that life can present to you. She once again reminds me that I am not alone. This book ended up being a ray of light to guide my way when I didn't even realize I was in need of some sunshine."

Lucy Calvillo, who will always believe in fairy tales in not-always-sunny San Diego

TURN
TOWARD
THE SUN

TURN TOWARD THE SUN

Releasing What If and Embracing What Is

MANDY HALE

Revell

a division of Baker Publishing Group
Grand Rapids, Michigan

Published by Revell
a division of Baker Publishing Group
PO Box 6287, Grand Rapids, MI 49516-6287
www.revellbooks.com

Printed in the United States of America

Library of Congress Cataloging-in-Publication Data
Names: Hale, Mandy, 1978– author.
Title: Turn toward the sun : releasing what if and embracing what is / Mandy Hale.
Description: Grand Rapids, MI : Revell, a division of Baker Publishing Group, [2022]
Identifiers: LCCN 2021050618 | ISBN 9780800738822 (paperback) | ISBN 9780800741976 (casebound) | ISBN 9781493436262 (ebook)
Subjects: LCSH: Attitude change—Religious aspects—Christianity. | Control (Psychology)—Religious aspects—Christianity. | Regret—Religious aspects—Christianity.
Classification: LCC BV4597.2 .H35 2022 | DDC 234—dc23/eng/20211130
LC record available at https://lccn.loc.gov/2021050618

The names and details of the people and situations described in this book have been changed or presented in composite form.

Published in association with The Bindery Agency, www.TheBinderyAgency.com.

Baker Publishing Group publications use paper produced from sustainable forestry practices and post-consumer waste whenever possible.

22   23   24   25   26   27   28   7   6   5   4   3   2   1

For my mom and dad . . .
My heroes, my best friends, my sunflowers,
the strongest people I know.
Thank you for showing me what true courage looks like
and for always reminding me to turn toward the sun.
I love you.

This book is in loving memory of my uncle
Vernie Hale
1949–2021

CONTENTS

Contents

INTRODUCTION

The book you're holding in your hands was supposed to be a different book.

It was supposed to be a very sassy, pithy book about letting go and moving on. If you've read my other books, especially my last book, *Don't Believe the Swipe*, and/or if you follow me on social media, you know *I love* sassy and pithy. And letting go and moving on are both topics I love to talk about. You don't make it to age forty-two as a single woman and not know a thing or two about letting go and moving on. Those are both really important concepts to explore, as I think most humans in general inherently struggle with letting go and moving on (especially those of us humans who happen to be anxiety-ridden control freaks). So I was excited to dive into a book *all* about letting go and moving on: from lost love, from toxic relationships, from dead-end careers, from one-sided friendships, from negative mindsets, etc., etc. And this book *will* cover some of those things.

15

But they're not the overlying themes of the book.
Why?

Because 2020 happened.

The dumpster fire that was 2020. The year that a global pandemic left us all *shook*. The year that racial injustice and political mayhem and social unrest raged. The year that found many of us quarantining alone for months on end. The year that the murder hornets came for us all. (And then left just as quickly because they read the room and decided that even they couldn't handle 2020.) The year that kept going . . . and going . . . and going. The year that left every person on the planet changed in one way or another.

It was also the year that both of my parents were diagnosed with cancer, one month apart from each other.

Even as I type that sentence, it still feels unreal to me. Sometimes, like right now, it hits me all over again that both of my parents, my best friends on this earth, have cancer . . . and I struggle to catch my breath. I find myself mentally bargaining: *Well, what if we could go back in time and change this? What if the doctor had found it sooner? What if none of this is even real and I wake up tomorrow and it's all just been a bad dream? WHAT IF, WHAT IF, WHAT IF?!*

I've always been obsessed with the idea of how things *could* be or *should* be. A girl with her head in the clouds. A dreamer. An idealist. A believer in magic. I've spent most of my life rejecting reality. I love movies and romance and Hollywood endings and happily ever afters. One could even argue that that's why I'm still single—because when you go through life expecting to find rom-com-level love on every corner, it can make real-life love seem . . . ordinary. Boring. Disappointing even.

I've also projected my great big, unrealistic expectations and *coulda woulda shoulda*s onto pretty much every other aspect of my life. I expect my friendships to look exactly like Monica, Rachel, and Phoebe's. I expect my writing career to mirror that of Carrie Bradshaw's. I expect family gatherings to be these grand Hallmark movie–level events, when in reality, they turn out to be much more National Lampoon–level fiascos. I have quite literally spent my life living in the *what if*. *What if* life was like this? *What if* love was like this? *What if* I was like this? So much so, that I have often overlooked and even downright ignored the *what is*. The *what is* being what is *really* happening. What my life really looks like. What actual love and not glittery love is supposed to look like. What real families and friendships and faith and feelings are made of instead of what TV and movies and books and everyone else's shiny social media posts tell me they should be made of.

And then 2020 happened. And then the pandemic happened. And then my parents' diagnoses happened.

And I couldn't live in Fantasyland anymore. Instead, I was brought crashing down to earth in a puddle of fear and grief and anxiety because this time, the *what is* was so big, I couldn't ignore it. I couldn't run from it. I couldn't deny it. I had to learn to live with it. And not just live with it but in it . . . and also somehow accept it and work with it and survive it and even thrive in the midst of it.

Perhaps the greatest irony of the whole thing is that for Lent 2020, I decided to give up . . . *control.*

For those of you not familiar with Lent, it's a Christian tradition in which you give up something—a bad habit, junk food, television, social media, etc.—for approximately forty days, or from Ash Wednesday until Easter Sunday. It's designed to imitate Jesus's fasting in the wilderness before He began His public ministry. I try to give up something every year in an effort to better myself, even if it's just Netflix or a sugary addiction. But in 2020, I decided to go big or go home and surrender control. As an admitted lifelong control freak, I felt like it was time to take my hands off the wheel for a while and let God take over. You know that old adage about if you want to make God laugh, tell Him your plans? Welp . . . I think in this instance, if you want to make God laugh, give up control in the year 2020, right before a global pandemic is unleashed into the world. I made my Lent resolution in February 2020. Exactly one month later, the entire world spun out of control.

And mine hasn't really stopped spinning since.

The thing is, you would think that when your world is spinning out of control, the best, smartest thing you could do would be to hold on even tighter.

But the thing you *actually* need to do . . . is learn to let go.

Let go into the grief, let go into the fear, let go into the sadness and anxiety and chaos and uncertainty. *Just let go.* Let yourself feel every last bit of it. Don't turn away from *what is* . . . turn toward it. Release your idea of what should be happening or could be happening or would be happening if things were only different and embrace what *is* happening. Even the big things. Even the scary things. Even the things you think you won't survive. Surrender control and just let go. Because the truth is, we're not in control of when global pandemics or illness or loss or heartbreak or even the really great big, amazing things in life happen. We're just not. We never were. If you're someone with anxiety, like me, reading that might be nerve-racking, even triggering. Those of us with anxiety like to constantly control our environments to protect ourselves from the unknown. The unknown terrifies us. We'd rather hide out in the safety of the *what if* than face the uncertainty of *what is*. But you want to know a secret?

The *what if* is where comparison and discontentment and bitterness and unhappiness happen. You're so stuck in wishing to be somewhere else, doing something else, with someone else, living someone else's life that you never learn to appreciate or value or even like your own life. You spend so much time glancing over the fence to where the grass is seemingly greener, your own lawn becomes neglected, uncared for, unattended, and overgrown with thistles and weeds. While the *what if* might feel warm and fuzzy and safe and secure for a little while, it's actually where dreams and happiness go to die.

But the *what is*? Yes, it might be where bad things and heartbreaking things and life-altering things sometimes happen . . . but it's also where immeasurably good things and breathtaking things and life-affirming things happen. Because your life, *just as it is*, the good and the bad, is precious, wild, wholly unique, and entirely worth embracing, celebrating, and living. *Just as it is.*

In the *what is*, you stop fighting against the wind and you learn to turn toward the sun. Did you know that when sunflowers are baby flowers, they physically turn toward the sun to help elongate their stems? In other words, turning toward *what is* and toward what's real—even when it hurts—actually helps you grow. And, yes, much like turning your face toward the sun on a hot summer day, accepting and learning to live in the *what is* might feel like trial by fire at

19

times . . . but it's where necessary growth and change and life happen.

The *what is* is also where you discover your own inner fire, your own courage, and your own strength.

I never considered myself a particularly strong woman. Even when I wrote blogs, tweets, and books encouraging other women to tap into their inner strength, I didn't really feel like I had mastered tapping into my own. I think, perpetually living in the *what if*, I was writing more about the self I wished I could be than the self I really was.

Then 2020 happened. A year that crashed into me and my family like a freight train. A year that would have left the Mandy from even one year earlier flat on her back on the floor.

But 2020 Mandy?

Yes, she might have doubted and feared and worried and wavered.

But eventually, she stood and she dealt. On her own, without anyone helping her up.

Yes, the princess rescues *herself* in this book.

I want to suggest to you today that perhaps you are a heck of a lot stronger than you think you are too. Perhaps you don't need or require a handsome prince to come along and hold your hand, dry your tears, and "rescue" you. Perhaps you were always meant to rescue yourself. Perhaps the happy ending was always going to be learning that only *you* are the author of it. Coauthors and costars and cosigners not required. Perhaps letting go of everything you think your life is supposed to be and embracing everything that it is—in all its messy, awful, beautiful, chaotic, heartbreaking, unexpected glory—is where your salvation and contentment and strength lay all along.

Because, truly, is there anyone better equipped than a single woman to roll with uncertainty and disappointment and unfulfilled dreams and life just plain not being what you want it to be? At age forty-two, I've had to surrender that idea of what I *thought* my life would look like and learn to accept and embrace it and even love it for what it actually *is*. Otherwise, I'd just be a miserable bitter Betty right now. Most of the friends I grew up with have high-school-age children right now and twenty-plus years of marriage under their belts. A few of them are even grandparents! And I've yet to even get started. So isn't singleness, in and of itself, a bit of a master class in learning to let go of the *what if* and live in the *what is*?

A couple of things before we get started.

First, a word on toxic positivity. In the past, I've been guilty at times of being a little too Miss Merry Sunshine when it comes to frantically searching for the silver lining of every single thing that's ever happened in life. I was so desperate to find meaning and purpose in the bad times, I would gloss right over the sheer weight of what was happening in order to try to make lemonade from lemons. As a result, I know I probably sometimes came off as glib or shallow or even just annoyingly chipper. But guess what? We're not going to do that in this book. Because there is no silver lining to cancer. Or pandemics. Or a lot of other horrible things that happen in life. And it's okay to acknowledge that and sit with the heaviness of it and not try to dismiss it with a trite "Everything happens for a reason." That may indeed be true, but has that sentiment ever really helped anyone? So, while I will be sharing stories from my life and lessons I've learned along the way in both bad and good times, I won't try to force you to find the good in every situation. Because in some situations, there simply is no good to be found. And I think it's healthy and necessary to admit that. It's also part of existing in the reality of *what is* instead of escaping into the fantasy of *what if*.

Second, my faith is very important to me, and I'll be talking about it throughout this entire journey but not in a "God works in mysterious ways and made that bad thing happen to make me stronger or to make you stronger" sort of way. I don't believe God makes bad things happen. I don't believe God is a God of bad things. I think bad things, like cancer and pandemics and divorce and wars and violence, happen separate from God, and while He doesn't cause these things, He does sit with us in the midst of them. There is not one single pain or fear or loss or tear we can experience that He has not experienced Himself. And isn't that kind of amazing when you think about it? That God doesn't run from your mess or condemn you for it but gets down with you in the trenches of it and holds you through every single second of it? That He wanted to be so close to us that He stepped into our skin to become one of us? That He needed to feel and experience the bittersweet journey of being fully human so we could never doubt that He knows what hurt and loss and disappointment and heartbreak feel like? And that He doesn't turn away from us, ever, for any reason? He turns toward us and accepts us and loves us not for who we could be or someday hope we will be but for exactly who we are.

So isn't it time for us to do that for ourselves?

I present to you now a collection of stories from my journey of being fully human. Times that stand out to me as examples of letting go of *what if* and surrendering to *what is.* Times when I chose to relentlessly turn toward the sun, no matter how many storms life threw at me. We'll be talking about a bit of everything here. Some of it bad, some of it good, some of it sad, some of it funny, some of it serious, some of it silly . . . but all of it real. I hope that along the way you will find a reflection of yourself in these pages. And I hope that reflection is one you'll embrace and appreciate and even love, regardless of how messy or imperfect or unfinished it might look to you. Because a wise woman once said, many moons and several books ago, that happiness is letting go of what you think your life is supposed to look like and celebrating it for everything that it is. (That wise woman, in case you haven't figured it out, was me.)

It is my prayer that this book will help you let go of *what if* and embrace *what is*, even when it's challenging, even when it's painful, even when it's scary, and even when it's sad. Because when you're feeling, you're growing, and when you're growing . . . you're living. And to live, to fully live, right smack-dab in the present moment, no matter what it may bring, is a beautiful thing.

Shall we get started?

1

It's the End of the World as We Know It

Day 6 of self-isolation: I just caught myself having a full-blown conversation with my cat. Send help.

I remember a time before the words *Covid* and *coronavirus* were a part of our daily vernacular. It's a distant memory . . . but it's a fond one.

In January or February of 2020, I started hearing whispers of these words on social media, faint at first. So faint, I paid them little attention and continued on about my life. The idea of a global pandemic shutting down society felt more like something from a movie than anything I thought I would ever experience in real life.

As February went on, the whispers grew a little louder. Covid was officially in the US, and the danger of it becoming a great big, major deal was growing exponentially every single day.

Day 8 of self-isolation: Might put on pants today.

I still didn't quite grasp what a "global pandemic" meant. I remember hearing all the rumors that the country was going to be shut down for a few weeks and we would all be on lockdown, and as someone who has a deep fondness for apocalyptic TV shows, books, and movies, I foolishly felt almost a little . . . excited? I realize how insane that sounds now, but remember: the emerging pandemic was on a scale that few people had seen in our lifetime, so how was I to know what we were up against? None of us knew. And I don't think any of us dared to imagine, even in our worst nightmares, the level of havoc and death and destruction Covid would ultimately go on to wreak on our country and our world. In my mind, I thought we'd all stay home for a couple of weeks, giving me an excuse to do two of my favorite things—watch movies and read—the threat would dissipate, and we'd all be back to business as usual. I think that's what most of us were thinking.

I remember going out to lunch one final time with two of my girlfriends in late February and, immediately afterward, going to the grocery store to stock up on food and prepare to batten down the hatches for a week or two. I had no way of knowing then that it would be the last time I would set foot in a grocery store for a year.

March 2020 arrived—a month that I am convinced will go down as the longest month in the history of the world—and the whispers became a shout. It was the end of the world as we knew it . . . and the reality of what was happening started to sink in. Schools closed. Businesses closed. People started working from home. Major world events, like the Olympics, started to get canceled or postponed, one by one by one. Covid officially arrived in Tennessee, where I live. The death toll began to slowly rise. Now the pandemic wasn't just a vague concern; it was a genuine threat. And my anxiety kicked in, hard core.

I've talked very openly about my anxiety on my blog, on my social media feeds, and in my books. I've suffered from anxiety for pretty much my entire life, and I've been diagnosed with panic disorder and generalized anxiety disorder. My anxiety is worse at some times than at others and is typically triggered by major life changes or events. It's also gone into what I think of as "remission" for years at a time, otherwise known as blissful seasons in which it will scarcely show its face. But in March 2020, it reared its ugly head in a whole new and uniquely awful manifestation—health anxiety. Suddenly everything and everyone seemed fraught with danger. Every sniffle and sneeze felt like coronavirus had invaded my body. Three other women and I lived in a house divided into apartments, which had always felt like a safe haven. Now it suddenly felt like a hotbed of germs. Could Covid be transmitted through the air vents? No one seemed to know. The *what if*s were absolutely terrorizing me. *What if I get Covid? What if I die? What if my parents get it? WHAT IF, WHAT IF, WHAT IF?!*

Day 10 of self-isolation: Today the tears came. And I'm letting myself have a good cry.

All of this might sound crazy to people who have never dealt with anxiety and/or panic attacks, but any situation with a perceived lack of control sends my anxiety spiraling. And what on earth could be less controllable than a deadly and highly contagious virus? Especially one we had never dealt with and that even the smartest and most educated scientists knew very little about. Every day I would wake up and monitor my body for symptoms. I checked my temperature at least five times a day. One morning, it was 99.1, and I was convinced the 'Rona had come for me. Panic became my moment-by-moment reality. The daily *what if*s were literally driving me crazy.

Day 13 of self-isolation: Today has been horrible, anxiety-wise. But I met with my therapist online earlier, wearing pajamas and crazy hair, and was met with nothing but calming reassurance. So onward we go.

As she usually does when I'm camping out in the *what if* and spiraling into an anxiety free fall, my wonderful therapist talked me down. "Mandy, you have to stop living to die and start living to *live*," she said. "You're taking all the precautions. You're being safe. You have to get out of the *what if* and live in the *what is*. Most of what you are worrying about will never happen."

We kicked up our biweekly sessions to weekly, a change that has remained in place to this day. And slowly, as she had advised, I began to pull myself out of the *what if* and come back to the *what is*. If you don't have a therapist, or if you don't have a good one, I can't recommend enough that you do some research and find someone you feel comfortable opening up to and allowing to speak into your life. Therapy has literally saved me, more than once. Even through a computer screen, my therapist was able to reach out and pull me out of a quickly spiraling black hole. Day by day, moment by moment, I started to accept and even acclimate to my new and unusual circumstances.

Day 23 of self-isolation: Feeling productive today. Might put on actual clothes and reintroduce myself to my bra today. (Or not.)

I didn't start marking my days of self-isolation on Twitter until Day 6—and I would go on to do so, every single day, until Day 100. Then I would continue to do so sporadically for the next 265 days, as my self-induced quarantine would go on to last the greater part of a year. When I say "self-isolation," I don't mean that I literally didn't see any humans or leave my house for a year. I saw my parents and my sister and her family, and I went to the bank and to the doctor and to the bookstore a couple of times, and I saw a few friends outside and from a safe distance. My parents and I even traveled to the Smoky Mountains in April 2020. So I didn't cut myself off from society and become the troll under the bridge. But I was about as cautious as a person could be.

A word to those of you who might think I was overreacting:

To some, Covid was no big deal. A lot of you probably went about your lives pretty much like normal. And that's fine, if that's what you felt led to do. Fine for you. For me, it was a very big deal. For one, we lost millions of people around the globe to this awful illness. I lost my great-aunt to it. I watched my cousins suffer her loss. I watched various social media friends grieve family members and other loved ones. I knew lots of other people who got very, very sick from it. So whether or not it happened to touch you personally . . . it was a big deal to me, and it was a big deal to countless others.

Aside from the obvious reasons why I was taking Covid so seriously, I wasn't eager to see how my anxiety and Covid would mix. Anything that makes me feel like I can't breathe can trigger a panic attack, meaning a disease like Covid is pretty much my worst nightmare come to life. And finally, my parents are my best friends and were my primary social circle throughout the pandemic. Though they wouldn't be diagnosed with cancer for six more months, I felt frantic to protect them from Covid, even without knowing how truly high-risk they were. I constantly scoped out eBay in search of disinfecting wipes, Lysol spray, masks, and gloves when they all became scarce on other platforms. I made sure my mom and dad had any and every supply they could possibly need to stay safe. And I admittedly, if somewhat ashamedly, joined in on the great toilet paper hoarding of 2020, stalking various online vendors for hours on end so I could snatch up rolls whenever they became available. (Something about running out of toilet paper made me feel especially anxious and vulnerable.) In other words, I was truly living my best life. (Pause here to note the obvious sarcasm.)

Day 38 of self-isolation: I just got toilet paper delivered, and I felt like a kid in a candy store, I was so excited!

Outside of my frantic toilet paper bingeing, I was starting to settle into a fairly content existence. My inner introvert had started to see the benefits of "normal" life coming to a grinding halt. Once I stopped scanning my body for Covid symptoms every day and stopped convincing myself that every sniffle or sneeze surely signaled the end for me, I looked around and realized that quarantine life was a little lonely, yes—but overall, surprisingly not so bad. No one else was really being super social during that time, so I didn't have FOMO (fear of missing out) when I would browse my social media platforms. I could wear lounge clothes all day, every day. I could catch up on that stack of unread books that was calling my name. I could bake and take naps and sit on my balcony and meditate and watch movies and color and basically do whatever I wanted. I had never felt more grateful for my career path than I did during those long months of solitude. I didn't have to show up to an office every day and worry about being exposed to a ton of other people. I didn't have to worry about getting laid off or furloughed like so many people did. My heart still bleeds for all the people who lost jobs and houses and life savings and career security and livelihoods during that uncertain time. Though I was dealing with my own fears and uncertainties and stressors, I knew how very fortunate I was, and it made me want to step out of the *what if* and into the *what is* even more. Gratitude will always pull you out of *what could have been* and plant you firmly into *what is* and *what could still be*.

About once a day, my downstairs neighbor would play her piano for thirty minutes or so. I would turn off my television and get super quiet so I could sit and listen to her play. She didn't know it at the time, but that quickly became my favorite part of the day. In those early days, I wasn't around anyone—even my parents—for weeks, so the sound of her fingers dancing across the keyboard became extremely comforting to me. I particularly enjoyed her rendition of "It Had to Be You." I think those are the moments from the early days of the pandemic that I'll look back on forever with such sweetness: that time in April 2020 when we were all weary and anxious and locked in our houses and still . . . the music played. God bless the creators.

God especially bless the creators who were able to continue creating during those weird days. I figured out quickly that while other people were "hustling and grinding" their way through the pandemic, I wasn't going to be one of those people.

Day 45 of self-isolation: I've made peace with the fact that I am not going to be that person who thrives in quarantine. I'm not going to start a podcast. I'm not going to lose twenty pounds. I'm not going to be the Moses of this operation and lead everyone out of the wilderness. And I'm okay with that.

A lot of people asked me, "Are you writing during this time?" And the answer was NO. I was barely even posting on social media. I had just finished a book. I knew I would be working on the next one (this one!) soon enough. I was just living. Breathing. Resting. Surviving. And I was completely at peace with that.

I knew someday I would be ready to write words again, and I hoped they would be good words and helpful words and meaningful words and deep words. But I also knew you couldn't have a story to tell if you didn't first live the story and survive the story. In spring 2020, I was living and surviving. It's okay if that's what you were doing too. It's even okay if that's what you're doing now. We all went through intense collective trauma for a solid year, and you don't just "bounce back" from that like you would a bad date or a rough day at work.

Sometimes, letting go of *what if* and learning to live in *what is* is about thriving. And other times it's about simply surviving. Learning to accept your circumstances with peace and finding contentment in the midst of the chaos doesn't mean you have to make friends with the chaos or be happy about the circumstances. I could be content with my life as it was in that season and still wish things were different. Same for you in whatever season you happen to be in right now. This is all part of what it means to turn toward the sun. It doesn't mean you have to turn every lemon into lemonade. It just means you have to learn to accept that lemons are an unavoidable part of life and deal with it. I honestly think sometimes it's a lot braver to learn to just sit with the lemons as they are rather than frantically try to turn them into lemonade.

If there was any lemonade that came out of the twilight zone known as the pandemic, I think it was that I learned, perhaps for the first time in my life, how to just . . . be. I gave myself permission to stop asking questions and stop searching for answers and stop making things happen and stop *doing, doing, doing* and *going, going, going*, and I learned how to just *be*. To be still, to be quiet, to be alone, to be content . . . with just me. No one else. Just me. It really is a beautiful thing learning to truly love and appreciate your own company. And I never would have done so had I stayed stuck in the endless rat race of *what if* instead of letting go into the uncertain peace of *what is*.

Did I want to essentially lose a year of my life to a pandemic? A year of dating? A year of fun times with friends? A year of taking trips and making memories with my family? No. And I would gladly hand back anything remotely positive that I gleaned from the pandemic if it meant getting that year back. But that's not how life works. And we can either be bitter about what was lost or be grateful for what still remains. What remained for me was an enduring ability to just let it be and live each moment as it happened rather than obsess about the past or stress about the future. That lesson would serve me well in the months to come.

Whatever it is you're going through right now . . . whatever it is you're enduring or muddling through or just simply trying to survive . . .

I want to give you permission . . . to just . . . be.

33

You don't have to be World's Best Mom or World's Best Employee or really World's Best anything.

You don't have to write an award-winning sonnet.

You don't have to tackle that spring cleaning or that big goal.

You don't have to be productive at all.

Maybe, in this moment, you don't have to solve anything or prove anything or figure anything out.

Maybe for right now, you can just let it all go. Let go of the endless *what if*s and relax into the *what is*—this present moment, reading this book, where you don't have to do anything other than just be.

Maybe what you need to do instead of moving forward frantically with no idea where you're headed is just be still.

Be angry if you need to be.

Be scared if you need to be.

Be honest.

Be lost.

Be uncertain.

Be whatever it is you are feeling without trying to put a happy sheen or a positive spin on it.

That's how you move on. That's how you survive. That's how you become.

Not by running in the endless hamster wheel of mindless productivity but by choosing to be at peace with whatever it is you need to do right now in this moment to get through this hard thing.

If that's not wearing pants for three days in a row . . . so be it.

If that's bingeing Netflix and eating ice cream . . . so be it.

If that's running five miles every day . . . so be it.

If that's shouting and screaming and cursing and punching pillows . . . so be it.

Just . . . let . . . yourself . . . *be.*

Whatever it is you're doing to get through the day right now . . . for now, it is enough. You are enough.

Take a deep breath, and let it be enough.

Take a deep breath, and let it be.

Take a deep breath, and just . . . *be.*

Day 365 of self-isolation: That's it. That's the tweet. Today marks one whole year of self-isolation.

As I write this, it's about fourteen months after March 2020, aka "the end of the world as we knew it." And I was telling my therapist just today that I feel like post-pandemic life is a bit like walking out of your house after a storm to find that everything has been completely leveled and you're left with a blank slate. Yes, we survived . . . but did anything from our previous lives make it out with us? As I look around, I'm not so sure yet. And in a way, that's terrifying. But in another way, it's incredibly exciting and even liberating. Can anyone else relate to that feeling? After a year of avoiding social contact and battening down the hatches and fighting to protect my high-risk parents from a deadly virus . . . after a year of just simply surviving . . . it's hard to figure out how to switch out of surviving mode into thriving mode. My social life has been impacted. My friendships have been impacted. (Some of them haven't survived at all.) My perspectives and mindsets on pretty much everything have been impacted. So where do we go from here?

Anywhere we want.

I want to invite you to shift your perspective today if you, too, feel like your life was leveled by the pandemic, or by anything else that came before it or during it or after it. What if we just start viewing whatever blank slate we've been given as a new beginning? A fresh start. A clean slate. To be whoever we want to be and do whatever we want to do and go wherever we want to go. None of us are the same people we were two years ago, or even a year ago, and that's okay. The storm might have taken a lot of things from us . . . but we are still here. To hope, to dream, to love, to live in the great big, beautiful mystery of *what still is*. To be the people we always wanted to be. Because sometimes the storm levels us.

And sometimes the storm helps us level up.

2

Where Were You When the World Stopped Turning?

My parents have always been my best friends. I know I'm lucky to be able to say that. I hold space and grace in my heart for people who aren't able to have that type of relationship with their parents, for whatever reason. I'm honestly not sure I would be as close with my mom and dad as I am if I had gotten married in my twenties or thirties like most of my friends did. But since I'm forty-two and still single, I've had the unique experience of watching our relationship transition from a parental bond to more of a friendship bond over the years. I hang out with them. I vacation with them. And during the pandemic, as my social circle grew smaller and smaller until it was pretty much nonexistent, they became my pandemic partners in crime. I felt this constant need to check in on them and take care of them and protect them. In hindsight, it's almost as though I knew I needed to. Maybe on some level, I sensed what was coming.

Since I am so close to my parents, and since I don't have a husband or kids of my own (yet), losing my mom and dad has always rated as pretty much number one on my list of biggest fears. As an anxiety sufferer and a worrier, I would constantly run the *what if* scenarios in my head every time they had even the slightest health issue pop up. *What if they have a serious illness? What if they get really sick or die? What if they leave me all alone? WHAT IF, WHAT IF, WHAT IF?!* I mean, obviously I know everyone is going to die *someday* . . . but I needed my parents' someday to be really, really far in the future. They are my family and my best friends, and I needed them here, with me, for as long as possible.

So in August 2020, when Dad was diagnosed with prostate cancer, it felt like the bottom dropped out of my world. He had been showing some symptoms, and we knew it was a possibility, but until you actually hear the words "I have cancer" from the mouth of someone you love, your mind can't begin to conceive the reality of what that means. Even when you do hear the words, your mind still can't conceive the reality of what that means. I was with Mom the day he got his results, both of us waiting on pins and needles to hear from him, and when he called with the news, all either of us could do was cry.

I remember when he got home that day, though it had been five long months since I had hugged anyone (due to the stupid pandemic), I rushed headlong into his arms and held on for dear life. I might have been forty-one years old, but he was my daddy and I needed him to be okay. I needed him to stay here, with me, for many more years to come. I needed him to walk me down the aisle someday and meet my future children and watch me realize all the dreams that I had had for myself and that he had had for me since I was a little girl.

The three of us sat and talked more about what Dad had learned from the doctor, and he started to tell me and Mom about what his treatment would look like. And as he did, I started to feel a little more hopeful. Though my *what if* brain had already leapt to the absolute-worst-case scenarios, I was relieved to hear that prostate cancer is something that most men will deal with at some point or another in their lives, and it's highly treatable. My dad had an excellent prognosis. The weight that had settled onto my shoulders upon hearing the awful C-word started to lift just a little. No, this wasn't what I wanted for my dad or for my family's journey at all, but it was what we had been given, and while it wasn't ideal . . . it could have been a whole lot worse. We could do this! I was a doer, a planner, a go-getter. I would read up on what kind of foods my dad needed to eat and what kind of vitamins he needed to take, and we would face down his radiation treatment together and beat this thing! Even though I was still shaken, I felt like we had been handed a manageable situation, and I just knew my family—and my dad—would win this battle.

Then, a month later, as we were preparing for the start of Dad's radiation regimen . . . the world came crashing down around all of us once again. This time, stronger and harder and more devastating than anything that had ever shaken our family before. Not even my darkest *what if* scenarios could have possibly conjured up the phone call we received on the night of September 18, 2020—my sister's birthday. That's the night that the phone rang, and on the other end was a doctor telling us my mom had metastatic cancer.

Two seemingly innocuous things led up to this phone call. First, my mom has pretty severe scoliosis, which led to her having intense back pain for as long as I could remember. Over the previous few months, it had gotten progressively worse, so she went in for an MRI to see what was going on and what she could do to alleviate the pain. And second, she had a tiny (benign, or so we had been assured by two different doctors) cyst removed from her side. We had no reason to believe that those things were connected or that they were anything to be concerned about. She had just had her annual physical in July and had been given a glowing and completely clean bill of health.

But then, around 7:30 p.m. on that September night, as I was hanging out with my parents like any other typical pandemic night, my dad's phone rang. It was the doctor who had removed the cyst and who also happened to be a family friend. We had been waiting for him to call with the results of the biopsy, slightly nervous about what he would say but not overly anxious. But as soon as I saw my dad's face, I knew the news was not good. And so did my mom.

Some moments in life are forever imprinted on our hearts and minds, and no amount of time or healing or therapy will ever erase them. That night was one of those moments for me—or, I guess, a series of moments. My mom's face. Her cries and screams as she realized what was happening. Her blue-and-white-checked pajamas. Me holding her as tightly as I could as my dad stepped out onto the deck to talk to the doctor. My heart hammering in my chest, which would normally trigger a panic attack for me . . . but that night, I felt completely numb. I felt no panic. I felt no sadness. I felt no fear or anger. I felt nothing. I was in shock. Which I'm honestly kind of glad about because it meant I was able to be there for my mom without regard for myself and what I was going through. I'm not grateful about many things having to do with that awful night, but I am so very thankful I happened to be at my parents' house on that night and in that moment for my mom. To hold her up, to comfort her, to let her know I was there, standing with her, and that we would find a way through this and that we would do it together. My sister cut her birthday dinner with her friends short to come be with us as we all fought to understand what was happening and why it was happening and what we were supposed to do next. The four of us huddled together, pandemic momentarily forgotten, and found solace in being near one another. The original four, like it was before my sister got married and had her own family. And it was just the four of us against the world.

My most feared *what if* in life had just become my *what is*.

When your most feared and dreaded *what if* suddenly, in one awful moment, becomes your *what is*, it feels like the world literally stops turning. Nothing makes sense. You can hear traffic going by and birds chirping and the news on TV droning on and on, and you know on some level that the world is still turning, like it always has and always will, but you want it to stop. You need it to stop. You need it to stop and take notice of the fact that nothing is right and everything is wrong and your heart is breaking and everything safe and warm and happy suddenly feels scary and cold and dark. You want to scream and cry and run away . . . far, far away from . . . yourself. And your life. And the phone call that just delivered a knockout punch to your soul. And everything, really. But you can't run from what's happening because wherever you go, there you are. And there *it* is. You can no longer hide out in the *what if* because the *what if* is suddenly the *what is*, and the *what is* has just shot you right through the heart and left you standing there bleeding. It's unfair and it's cruel and it's devastating and it's excruciating, but it's your new reality, and you can either run and hide in the corner and deny what's happening . . . or you can stand, and you can deal.

I stood, and I dealt.

I stood with my mom that night and physically held her up as she cried and grieved. I stood with my dad as he came back inside and tearfully relayed to us his discussion with the doctor—how he knew from the biopsy that it was metastatic cancer, but he didn't know yet what kind. In the coming days, I would stand with my family as Mom faced test after test to pinpoint exactly what was happening in her body. And finally, I stood with myself, as the months ahead would be the hardest and loneliest and most challenging I had ever known. My anxiety would try, time and time again, to come in and take over, and time and time again . . . I refused to let it.

That night, before I left Mom and Dad's to head home, Mom was fretting and worrying about what kind of cancer she had. "It must be all over me," she cried. I held her close and whispered in her ear: "Tonight, it's not all over you. Tonight, we don't know exactly what we're dealing with, so it's not all over you. Just for tonight, let's hold tight to that.

Tomorrow will bring what tomorrow brings. But tonight, let's hold on to hope."

Where did my calmness come from in the face of such devastation? I had reacted in a similar way a few years prior, when my brother-in-law was in a near-fatal car wreck and lost his leg. No tears, no panic attacks . . . just complete and total calm. I think—and this is just my theory—that anxiety-ridden people are always so busy living in the *what if* and mentally preparing for the absolute-worst-case scenario that when the worst actually *does* happen, we almost . . . weirdly . . . relax. It's kind of like if you've been preparing for months and years for "The Big One" earthquake: running drills, purchasing supplies, making sure you know exactly where to go and what to do when and if it hits. Then when it does strike and tries to shake you to your very core, you're able to hold it together and stand strong because you've been preparing for this day for years while everyone else laughed at you for even worrying about such a thing. That's the best analogy I can come up with for why anxious people seem to fall apart in the face of imagined danger and yet hold it together in the face of actual danger. Not to say I wouldn't have lots of shaky days and depressed days and anxious days and just plain bad days ahead of me—because I would—but in that moment on that terrible night, I was unshakable. I was an anxiety-ridden person who felt ill-equipped to face most hard things, but I was still standing after the most crushing blow of my life. And I'd still be standing twenty-four hours later. And I'm still standing today, as I write this, almost nine months later. Maybe, just maybe . . . I'm stronger than I ever realized.

Or maybe I just learned somewhere along the way to let go of *what if* . . . and embrace *what is*.

(Or maybe it's a little bit of both.)

When you're dealing with cancer, you have no choice but to let go. To let go of control, to let go of the idea that you can do anything at all to change things, to let go of all the other little inconsequential worries and fears that once took up so much space in your brain. It's *cancer*. The Big Bad Wolf of worries and fears. And when you're dealing with the Big Bad Wolf on a daily basis already, you no longer have the energy to conjure up endless "What if the sky is falling?" scenarios because *the sky is actually falling* and you're fighting every second just to keep holding it up and being there for the people you love. You have to let go, every single day, and surrender control to a Higher Power because there is not one single, solitary thing you can do to control cancer, to change cancer, or to make cancer go far, far away from you or the person you love.

But here's a secret that I hope will help set you free a little bit. Are you ready?

There's not much you can do to control *life* either.

(Did you hear that? I believe it was a truth bomb falling from the sky and landing on this page.)

We can't control life. We can't control disease and illness. We can't control pandemics. We can't control who becomes president. We can't control how people feel about us. We can't control how people treat us. We can't control other people at all. We can't control our singleness or when or if we'll get married (Lord knows, I've tried!). We can't control traffic or weather or lost luggage or delayed flights. We can't stop bad things from happening. We can't stop the people we love from getting sick. We can't stop death. We just simply *can't*. It's not in our power. Yes, we can control how we choose to live our lives, but we cannot and will not ever be able to control life itself. So you might as well stop trying because it's doing nothing but making you crazy and making you anxious and making you stressed and, honestly, probably making that life you're trying so hard to control a whole lot shorter and infinitely less peaceful and happy.

If you're anything like me, you're probably thinking, *But if I admit that I'm not in control and I just let go, I'm opening up the door to anxiety and depression and sadness and worry and fear.*

And to that I say—IT'S OKAY.

It's really, really okay to let yourself feel sad sometimes. Or scared sometimes. Or vulnerable sometimes. Or even depressed sometimes. Or whatever it is you need to feel sometimes. I've had to give myself permission to feel sadness because, when you've dealt with depression, any trace of sadness can feel like it's going to take you under. But here's the thing: If you never allow yourself to feel—to really *feel* the full range of wildly fluctuating human emotions—you might not ever feel sad, but you won't ever feel happy either. They're kind of like flip sides of the same coin. Or like a "two for the price of one" set of emotions. One cannot exist without the other. And part of letting go and admitting and embracing not being in control is allowing yourself to fall apart and into whatever feeling it is your body and heart need to feel. Let yourself be a mess for a little while. Let yourself cry. Scream. Cuss. Punch a pillow. Even ask God "*Whyyyyyy?*" To live, to truly live, means you will experience it all: The dark and the light. The day and the night. The smiles and the pain. The sunshine and the rain. So let it all happen to you. And don't be afraid. Or do be afraid.

But know that even afraid, you can do this. Whatever your "this" is. You can survive this. You *will* survive this. One step at a time, one moment at a time.

That's the other half of learning to turn toward the sun—not just letting go of the perceived control of the *what if* but also embracing the certain uncertainty of the *what is*. Especially when the *what is* is not what you want it to be. Every day since September 18, 2020, I've had to learn how to exist in the present moment and let go of what happened yesterday or what's coming tomorrow. Trying to live in anything other than the present moment is just too overwhelming and exhausting. We faced doctor's appointment after doctor's appointment and test after test for weeks on end. And we were doing it all in the midst of a pandemic, which made everything a million times more stressful than it already was. I could drive Mom and Dad to the doctor, but I wasn't allowed to go in with them. I can't tell you how many days I sat in the car, waiting . . . just waiting . . . for results and news and diagnoses, and for a verdict on what the next three months, six months, year of our lives was going to look like. And every moment that ticked by as I sat there in that vulnerable space of waiting—stuck between what had been and what would still be—I had to, over and over again, *choose* to sit right there in the tension of that moment without wasting my time trying to wish it away or worrying about what was coming next. One step at a time, one moment at a time, one day at a time was all my family and I could do. That's how we would get through this. That's how we would win this battle. There's even a Scripture that addresses this perfectly: "Give your entire attention to what God is doing right now, and don't get worked up about what may or may not happen tomorrow. God will help you deal with whatever hard things come up when the time comes" (Matt. 6:34). I couldn't waste my time fretting about tomorrow's results before we even got through today's test. I couldn't fully be there for Mom and Dad and offer the support and the love they needed if I was constantly stuck in the whirlwind of my own anxious thoughts.

I came to realize in those early days of my family's fight that this journey was a marathon, not a sprint, and it was teaching me every day to live in the moment and be grateful for small mercies without worrying too much about what tomorrow would bring. It's a lesson I'd have been grateful to hand back if it meant we could undo everything that had happened since September 18, 2020—or heck, even all of 2020! But that's not how life works. Life isn't like that infamous episode of *Dallas*, and I knew I wasn't going to wake up and find Bobby Ewing in my shower and realize that it had all been a bad dream. The year 2020 was awful for a lot of us, and it left all of us changed forever in small ways and big ways, and the truth is, I didn't have any magic words or a catchy quote to change that or make it better. All I had in that moment was my faith and my family and my hope that better days were coming . . . for my parents, for me, for all of us. And in that moment, that was enough.

3

Have We Met Before?

We'll come back to my parents' story and my family's journey through cancer, but I wanted to lighten things up for a moment and tell you about a time when I had a serendipitous encounter with someone who taught me a wonderful lesson about letting go of the *what if* and embracing the *what is*. I'm not entirely sure this person wasn't an angel. There have been times when I've crossed paths at precisely the right moment with someone who said something that made me think or that helped me see the world or myself in a different light. You might have heard of moments like these referred to as "God winks." I love God winks, and I'm always amazed and even enchanted by those moments when someone appears in my life just to teach me a lesson or share a bit of wisdom, only to then leave just as quickly as they arrived.

If you've read my second book, *I've Never Been to Vegas, but My Luggage Has,* you might remember the story of my high school sweetheart, Matt. Matt and I started dating at the beginning of our senior year and were together for about three years, all told. On that terrible night in September 2020 when we got the call about my mom, Matt was the first person I called after I got home. I spent that sleepless night staring at the ceiling, terrified that both of my parents were going to die but still not able to let go and let myself cry. I felt empty and scared and alone. So I did what I always do when life punches me in the gut. At some point in the middle of the night, I picked up the phone and I called Matt.

And he did what he always does. He answered my call.

I guess there are just some people in the world whose hearts are tied together by an invisible thread, no matter how much time or space or distance might separate them. Matt is one of those people for me. I know I could call him anytime, on any day, for any reason, and he would pick up the phone. Just as he's been picking up the phone for me for the past twenty-five years. And I would do the same for him. It's no longer a romantic connection that we share, but it's a soul connection . . . one that is just as significant as any romantic connection I've ever had. Perhaps even more so. (Funny story: I heard from Matt as I was writing this chapter. We hadn't spoken in almost a year, and a few hours after completing this chapter, my phone lit up and there he was, in another wonderful little God wink. Soul connections are such a funny, wonderful part of life. Okay, carry on.)

You may also recall from *Never Been to Vegas* that Matt faced—and won—his own battle with cancer when we were in our late twenties. And I stood by him through it, even sitting with him through chemo treatments even though I had another boyfriend at the time. Matt also knows and loves my parents. So I knew if anyone could find a way to meet me right in the middle of my heartbreak in that moment, it would be Matt. And he did, like he always does.

But, to tell the story I want to tell about Matt, we have to turn back the clock about twenty-four years to just after our high school graduation. Matt joined the Marines, active duty, right out of high school, which meant he was gone almost all the time, with only brief weekend visits here and there. He would come home, I would be thrilled to see him, our precious time together would fly by . . . then it would be time to take him back to the airport and cry my eyes out all the way back home. I was only nineteen years old, so having a boyfriend who was home maybe only two or three times a year was heart-wrenching.

On one such occasion, Matt's best friend and I had taken him to catch his flight back to the base. Remember, back in those days, you could walk someone all the way to their gate and even sit with them until their plane arrived, which is what I normally did, soaking up every single second with him. On this particular night, however, I was having an especially hard time with Matt leaving. I was riddled with anxiety, I couldn't stop crying, and I felt dangerously close to a panic attack. I was nineteen years old, aka self-conscious, insecure, and completely clueless about life in general. It would take years before I was comfortable enough with myself not to care what people thought of me, and on that night, I was super embarrassed at the thought of having a complete emotional meltdown in front of Matt, his best friend, and the entire airport. I was so stuck in the *what ifs*, I couldn't let myself just sit and soak in the *what is* of my last few moments with the man I loved. So I said my farewells quickly and made up some excuse about why I needed to leave before his plane took off. Matt looked surprised, and maybe even a little hurt, but he hugged me tightly for a minute and we said a quick goodbye. Instead of leaving, though, I stopped at an airport coffee shop to catch my breath, tears blinding my vision. My heart was pounding, I was shaking, and I knew a panic attack was imminent. In my mind, Matt seeing me like that was worse than my not seeing him for as long as I possibly could.

The airport coffee shop was almost empty, except for an older gentleman sitting by himself at a table in the corner. I took a seat at a table next to his, wanting to be alone with my thoughts but still wanting the comfort of someone's presence there with me since I was a ball of nerves. Somehow, letting a stranger see me like this was preferable to letting my longtime boyfriend see me like this. (Anyone who has ever been a teenager will understand that sentiment.) I was sobbing, reliving the past few days with Matt, and wondering how long it would be before I would get to see him again. I was also beating myself up for being so weak and letting my anxiety completely control me and cause me to walk away from Matt instead of standing by his side until the last possible second.

"Are you okay, little miss?" A kind, quiet voice shattered my rumination.

I looked up from my soggy tissue. It was the old man at the table next to me. He was wearing a fedora-type hat and a trench coat, which felt like an odd ensemble for an indoor airport coffee shop.

"Oh, yes sir . . . I'm fine," I replied, wiping my eyes. "I'm just a little sad because I just had to say goodbye to my

51

boyfriend. Well, his plane doesn't leave for another hour or so, but I went ahead and said goodbye because I'm just having such a hard time with letting him go. I didn't want to draw things out and start blubbering and making a scene." I had no idea why I kept rambling on, as I'm sure the man was just being polite and didn't want or need to hear my life story. But something about his presence was calming and comforting, and I instantly felt like I could tell him anything. Already, my panic had started to subside, and I felt less shaky and alone.

I stopped my incessant babbling for a moment and looked more closely at the man. "I'm sorry, but have we met before? You look . . . familiar."

The man smiled. "No, I don't think so. But I hear that a lot." He handed me a fresh napkin to dry my face. "Don't you think you ought to go back and be with your boyfriend until his plane takes off? Savor every moment you have with him? I know that's what I would do."

I sat and pondered that for a moment. "But what if I start bawling or have an emotional breakdown and I embarrass him?" I asked. "Isn't it better that I just say my goodbyes to him calmly and rationally and then come sit here in this empty coffee shop and bawl and embarrass only myself?"

The old man laughed. "Ah. You worry too much about *what if*. I say focus on *what is*! And *what is* here . . . is clearly love. I'm pretty sure if this young man loves you like I can see you love him, he can handle a few tears." He chuckled again. "And I bet he'd welcome that emotional breakdown if it meant spending a few more minutes with you."

I began to smile through my tears. The old man was right. What was I doing? Why was I letting the *what if* rob me of the *what is*? Why was I missing out on precious time with the man I loved with my whole heart in the name of . . . neatness? Of politeness? Isn't love supposed to be messy and colorful and wonderful and beautiful and magical and inconvenient and wildly outside the lines? And if our love could handle the constant separation we had already endured, couldn't it certainly handle a few tears? Maybe even a little snot? Or even, possibly, a hugely public and embarrassing panic attack?

I hurriedly stood up, dabbed my eyes with the napkin, and turned to the old man.

"You're right. You're absolutely right! I'm going to go back and sit with him until his plane leaves. Thank you so much! Thank you for helping me see what is right in front of my face."

The old man smiled. "My pleasure, young lady. Godspeed to you both."

I rushed out of the coffee shop and back into the crowded airport to go find my love and sit with him until it was time for him to go. Because that's what love does. It doesn't let *what if* stand in the way of *what is*. It doesn't bail and check out early because the ending is a little messy. Love stays until the very end. Until the last page. Until the credits roll. It doesn't take the easy way out, and it doesn't go hide in a corner out of fear. It doesn't go halfway. It goes all the way, every single time. It doesn't show up just for the beautiful beginning but also for the bittersweet end. Love is all in without fear of anything, including any *what if* you could ever throw at it.

It took a kind old man in a fedora and a trench coat in an airport coffee shop to remind me of that.

I glanced back one last time to smile and wave at the man before the coffee shop was out of sight.

He was gone.

———

Just be yourself. In life and, especially, in love. Let people see the real, imperfect, flawed, quirky, weird, beautiful, magical person you are. It is enough. You are enough. Don't let fear or worry or messiness or insecurity or any *what if* you can possibly think of rob you from one single second of living in the *what is* with the people you love. Life is so very precious. If the past few years have taught us nothing else, they've taught us that.

I think the man in the fedora would agree.

4

An Endless Night . . . and Then, the Sun

The night we got the news about my mom and I went home and called Matt in the wee hours of the morning was by far the worst night of my life. I didn't sleep a wink that night. I lay there going over everything in my mind—all the millions of *what ifs*—trying to make it all make sense. As a doer, I was desperate to find a way out, a way through, a way past this nightmare my family and I were now trapped in. In those late-night hours, I ordered a video camera from Amazon so I could start capturing precious moments with Mom and Dad, just in case. I prayed. And when I say I prayed, I mean I talked to God and questioned God and yelled at God. I knew He could handle it. I paced the floors. I went over in my mind everything we knew so far and everything we didn't know, and then I went over it all again at least a dozen times. And by the time the sun rose the next morning, my face was set like flint, my spine like steel. I wasn't going to just roll over and let this awful disease take my parents away from me. I was ready to help them take on this battle and do whatever we had to do to win it. Of course, I had no real control over what was going to happen. But in those eight or ten sleepless hours, as I lay there formulating a plan to defeat cancer, I convinced myself that I did.

Every day my parents' van became my own compact waiting room, and every moment became an exercise in letting go and surrendering to God. What else could I do? I wasn't even allowed to accompany them into the doctor's office due to Covid. It was such a helpless feeling.

I had zero control over anything that was happening, and more than once, my Lent offering of surrendering control came back to haunt me. Had I caused all this? In trying to give up my control-freak ways, had I unleashed all this uncontrolled chaos on my family? Of course I hadn't, but it was hard not to feel guilty for anything and everything. Anyone who has ever had a family member diagnosed with cancer or another serious illness can relate to that feeling, I'm sure. You feel guilty for any mean thing you've ever said to the person who's suffering. You feel guilty for being healthy when they're not. You feel guilty for not doing enough to help them, and no matter how much you do, it never feels like enough. Of course, this guilt is just another way the *what if* keeps us trapped. When we're stuck in our own heads and playing a broken record of guilt over and over on repeat, we've stepped out of *what is* and into *what if*. And that is one song that remains the same, no matter how many times you replay it.

Within a couple of weeks, we had an official diagnosis. Mom had lung cancer, and it had spread to her spine. My mom, who had never smoked a day in her life. My mom, who hates cigarettes and everything associated with them. The news was devastating. It felt like a cruel joke.

But we had prayed fervently and had everyone around us praying fervently, asking God to please just give us a fighting chance and a little bit of hope . . . and He delivered on both.

We soon learned that Mom was one of only 5 percent of all people with her type of cancer who could take a chemo pill instead of having to undergo traditional chemotherapy. Five percent!!! She would have to go through radiation, which would prove to be extremely rough on her body, but once she was done with that, instead of having to go right into chemo treatments, she would be able to stay home and take a daily pill. It was such a great big, gigantic blessing from God. The pill had very few side effects, and she wouldn't get sick or lose her hair. All I could do the day we got that news from her oncologist was fall to my knees, weeping, and praise God. This journey was awful, and I wouldn't wish it on my worst enemy, but grace and mercy were falling on us with every step we took. I found myself drenched in gratitude. And that's when I learned, perhaps for the first time in my life, how much of an optimist I really am. As I mentioned earlier, I've always been a dreamer and an idealist, but my anxiety has at times caused me to look at life from a glass-half-empty perspective and assume the worst is going to happen. But something about the worst *actually* happening—my mom and dad both having cancer—brought out the optimist in me, along with my need to turn toward the sun instead of away from it. I heard the positive in everything the doctor told us. Every time Mom completed another day of radiation, I saw it as one step closer to our goal. Every day, I would march into Mom and Dad's house with my game face on. "We're in the home stretch now!" I would say to Mom as we readied her for that day's treatment. I remained doggedly positive for the first two months after her diagnosis. I just knew we were going to cross all the hurdles and win all the battles and get Mom and Dad both back to full and complete health. Dad's prognosis was good, and while Mom's was a little more uncertain, her doctor thought she had a really good shot at remission. So that became my goal, and I became quite single-minded in pursuing that goal.

The radiation treatments were incredibly intensive and painful and hard on Mom. Her anxiety was at an all-time high, and her spirits were at an all-time low. And I can understand that now, several months removed from it. At the time, though, I was frustrated. I wanted her to catch the vision that I had. I wanted her to put her game face on! I wanted her to show cancer who was BOSS!

But here's the thing: I wasn't the cancer patient; she was. I was her daughter and, yes, I was hurting and sad and grieving her diagnosis right along with her, but I wasn't living her diagnosis. I wasn't walking in her shoes. I wasn't the one who got that horrible news just two months after being told I was perfectly healthy. I wasn't the one having to show up to radiation treatments every day, lie on a hard table, and endure an hour of being moved and stretched and poked and prodded on my already sore back as they found the right angle and position to fire the lasers. My life had been shaken to the core, but I hadn't had the rug completely ripped out from under me the way my mom had. Her husband had cancer, and now she had even-more-serious cancer. Who was I to tell her to get her game face on? It was just another way I was trying to control an uncontrollable situation. I had good intentions, but I was letting my anxiety and need to control things try to control *her* and how she dealt with the most earth-shattering, life-altering news any human could ever get. I had fallen back into *what if* thinking, and I was letting my *what if* control her *what is*. And it wasn't my place to do that.

I was back on a crash course of *doing, doing, doing,* and I wasn't yet ready to acknowledge my mistakes. It would take a full two months for my crash course . . . to become my crash.

I downloaded healing Scriptures and affirmations and laminated them for Mom and Dad. I researched and made them foods that were good for cancer patients to eat. I bought a blender and started whipping up protein smoothies for Mom every day. I played healing meditations for her while I rubbed her feet. I helped her do her hair when she grew weak from radiation. I cooked and cleaned and did laundry and ran errands and crammed their freezer so full of healthy frozen meals, there wasn't an inch of space left for anything else. I was frantic, almost manic, in my need to keep moving. I needed to do, to act, to plan. I couldn't let myself stop moving even for a moment because, if I did, the reality of what we were going through would catch up to me, and I wasn't ready to deal with the reality of the *what is* just yet. The *what if* felt much safer to me in those hard days. *What if I find a way to fix all this? What if I make sure they eat nothing but healthy food all the time? Maybe that will somehow reverse the cancer. What if I miraculously cure Mom with this peanut butter protein smoothie?!* It was insane, I know

59

. . . but in that moment, I was grieving and scared and desperate to find something, anything, I could control so that the giant EF5 tornado we were swirling around in would let us go and let us be.

And then, in November, on the day before Thanksgiving, Mom got sick. Really sick. She was fine one day, and the next she wasn't. She was lethargic and her breathing was labored and her oxygen levels were dropping quickly. She was so weak, my dad and I had to work together to bundle her up and get her to the car so we could rush her to the hospital. I was fighting a massive panic attack the entire time, my heart pounding through my chest. It was one of the most terrifying moments of my life.

When we got to the hospital, because of Covid, once again I had no choice but to drop them off at the door and sit in the car. Sit and wait and worry. We didn't know if, despite our overabundance of caution, Mom had somehow contracted Covid or if it was something else going on altogether. And we wouldn't know for twelve more hours, when her Covid test mercifully came back negative. The doctor explained that lung cancer patients often suffer bouts with pneumonia, particularly after radiation treatment, which can cause the lungs to puff up and fluid to gather there. Mom had a nasty case of pneumonia, and all we could do now was wait for the antibiotics to work. And pray. And pace. And worry. I did an abundance of all of the above over the next several days, as she remained in the hospital for a week.

Thanksgiving Day 2020 found me sitting at Mom and Dad's kitchen table, by myself, halfheartedly eating the warmed-up Thanksgiving dinner I had preordered for us a few days earlier. Dad was with Mom at the hospital around the clock, but I could only be there for short amounts of time due to pandemic restrictions. And I couldn't go be with my sister and her family, as my sister was a teacher and around germs all day long and I didn't want to risk carrying something back to Mom when I did get to visit her. So, for the first time in my life, I was alone on a holiday. Something in me broke that day. All I could do was look around the empty seats at the table and cry as I pictured us all seated together at our last Thanksgiving dinner, laughing and bickering and eating and going around the table to share what we were grateful for. It had been imperfect, as every gathering with my family (or any family, for that matter) tends to be . . . but we had been together. Why hadn't I treasured that togetherness more when I had it? Now I felt like an island, floating alone in the middle of an abyss, tethered to nothing and no one. My parents were sick, and I was alone.

In that moment, I came face-to-face with the fact that I didn't have control over anything that was happening.

I had held on so tightly for months to the *what if*—in this case, *What if I could do things differently or better and magically make my parents not be sick?*—that when I finally had to sit down and have a reckoning with the *what is*, I felt flattened. The reality was, my parents were sick and there was nothing I could do to make it stop. There was nothing I could do to make it better. There was nothing I could do at all. I felt so weak and so helpless and so scared. I remember the morning after Thanksgiving, as I was taking a bath and trying to get ready to tackle another day, I didn't feel like I had the energy to wash my face. The idea of another day spent contending with the hospital and cancer and anxiety and the unknown of everything that was happening felt like too much to bear.

Then I picked up my phone and mindlessly scrolled through Twitter. One stranger said something kind and another sent prayers and well wishes and still another one tweeted me a funny, silly meme. My friends knew what I was going through with my family, and they were there for me in their own unique virtual way. In those small and random acts of kindness, I found the glimmer of strength I needed to get through another day, and I found the courage to turn away from the shadows and turn back toward the sun.

So now I want to say this to you, hopefully to help you find the spark you need to get through another day and find your way back to the sun: I don't know what you're dealing with. I don't know what your burden or your cross to bear is in this life. Or crosses to bear. I don't know what you're trying to control or what great big *what if* you're facing or what life-altering *what is* you've been dealt or are currently running from . . . but I do know this: You can let go. You must let go. Drop your arms, drop your pride, drop your endless questions and your need to know all the answers right now, drop your desire to control, and just let go. Clinging to the idea that you alone hold the power to heal someone or fix something broken or make something play out differently than it's going to play out is futile, and it's exhausting, and it's unfair to you and whoever it is you're trying to save. You can't save people. You can only love them through whatever battle they're facing and vow to march shoulder-to-shoulder with them as they face it. Trust me when I say this: Just being there with someone and *for* someone, in the middle of their hurt and their pain and their mess and their sickness and their heartbreak, is worth more and makes more of a difference than a million protein shakes. You don't always have to be doing something to be there for someone. The most active verb in the English language is *love*. Your loving them is enough. It is everything.

And here's some more good news:

If your heart is broken, I want you to know that Jesus is right there with you in the midst of it. You can cry out to Him, even if you have no one else on this earth who you feel like you can talk to. Even if you're as alone and bereft as I felt on that terrible Thanksgiving Day. He is closer than your next breath. He hears your every heartbeat. The Bible tells us He catches every tear you cry in a bottle (Ps. 56:8 NLT). He knows, He understands, He is there with you in the suffering. We do not have a far-off God who sits on a pedestal and knows nothing of pain. We have a God who chose to become human and to come down and join us in the midst of our mess. The Bible says Jesus is a man of sorrows and acquainted with grief (Isa. 53:3 NLT). He knows what a broken heart feels like. And He will walk with you through every moment of the sadness if you'll let Him. God always hears a broken heart. When our eyes are so clouded by tears that we can't see our next step, we can cling to that beautiful truth.

When I finally broke, it was the start of my new beginning. Once I finally admitted I was powerless and surrendered control of both the *what if* and the *what is* to God, I was able to walk through the fire with a much greater peace. My mom would get out of the hospital. She would go on to continue her fight against cancer. So would my dad. Mom completing her radiation, then Dad completing his. We would experience ups and downs and highs and lows, and we would all learn to ride the roller coaster of cancer with a little more grace and a little more acceptance. That Christmas would find us celebrating with my sister and her family through a computer screen, all of us crying, wishing we could be together, but able to find deep, rich gratitude for the fact that we were all still here. And, yes, we would have anxious days and hard days and sad days ahead of us, but we would also find reasons to smile and laugh and celebrate. Like when we got Mom's first scans back, postradiation, and the tumors had shrunk more than 30 percent. Or when Dad rang the bell to mark his final day of treatment. Or when I wrote an article that appeared in *USA Today*. Or when the team we were rooting for on *Family Feud*, my mom's favorite game show, won. Life can still be good when you are determined enough to look for the sun. And we were.

As I write this, Dad is completely done with his cancer treatment, and Mom is doing better than ever. Each day she gets a little stronger and seems a little bit more like her old self. That is our *what is* today. Who knows the *what ifs* we might face tomorrow? None of us do. And honestly, none of us need to. Today is what matters. And today we choose to let go, march forward, and keep stubbornly turning toward the sun.

I hope you will too.

5

How I Lost Love and Found Myself

We've talked a bit about my first great love, Matt, but I'd like to introduce you to my last great love . . . or at least, my last love. In hindsight, I'm not sure I'd call him a "great love." I think to qualify as a great love, the person has to stick around for longer than three or four months, and by that measure, this guy doesn't meet the criteria. He was in and out of my life like a flash in the pan, but I felt the burn of his abrupt departure for months after he left. Although I touched on this relationship a little bit in my last book, *Don't Believe the Swipe*, I didn't go into great detail about it because I didn't feel far enough removed from it to write about it yet. For the purposes of the story, we'll call this guy . . . Berger. As in Jack Berger, from *Sex and the City*. I like to name the exes I talk about in my books after characters from TV shows I love, and Jack

Berger feels fitting here. My ex didn't break up with me on a Post-it, like Berger did Carrie, but he *did* break up with me in a five-minute-long phone call, which isn't that much different from a Post-it. Anyway . . . my relationship with Berger was brief, but it taught me so much about letting go of what I thought I wanted out of love. Because, you see, with Berger I found what I thought I had been looking for my entire life. And as it turned out, what I thought I had found and what I *actually* found were two different things. As were what I thought I wanted and what I actually needed and deserved. But I'm getting ahead of myself. Let me back up to the beginning of the story.

A few years ago, I met a guy. I had put myself out there and taken a chance on dating apps and, against all odds, found someone who I felt was special. Quickly. Very quickly. (Some might say too quickly.) We started dating, and it took a serious turn pretty rapidly. I knew when I broke my first-date rule by letting him give me a good-night kiss at the end of our first date that I was probably getting ahead of myself. But it just felt so good to connect with someone again and to feel all the sparks and butterflies and excitement that come along with that connection. (If you're out there in the dating world and on dating apps, I'm sure you know how very rare this kind of connection is.)

In the first week or so of dating, however, Berger lied to me about something pretty significant. The details don't really matter, but what does matter is that I felt completely betrayed and confused. My mind was spinning with *what ifs*: *Was this a one-time mistake, or can this guy not be trusted? What if I give him a second chance and he hurts me worse down the line? What if he cheats on me? What if I end up completely heartbroken because I didn't heed what must surely be a great big red flag?* He *had* admitted to the lie, which seemed to point to the fact that perhaps he had just made an error in judgment and wasn't a serial liar. After a long conversation with him, I decided not to let all my *what ifs* destroy what seemed to be the beginnings of a great love story. I gave him a second chance, and at first the fact that we had worked through something so intense so early on and had come out on the other side seemed to make us stronger.

I went on to fall in love with this man who I thought for a brief moment might be my forever. And this was hugely significant, as it was the first time I had fallen in love in at least a decade. It was the first time I had ever talked marriage with someone in a real, tangible way. It was the first time I had ever seriously dated someone with a child. He had a little girl whom I quickly came to love as much as I loved him. I remember one night we were all sitting together in his living room, Berger and his daughter and me, and I looked around and realized that I suddenly had everything I had ever wanted. Right in front of me, painting a beautiful picture of the innermost desires of my heart come to life, was the man I loved and a little girl I adored. A built-in, ready-made family. How had I gotten so lucky?

The fact that Berger seemed determined to move at warp speed didn't concern me, at least not at first. I believed I had stumbled into one of those magical "When you know, you know" love stories, where all the pieces fall together effort-lessly and it doesn't require months or years to decide you are meant for each other. In hindsight, I can see the red flags a lot more clearly. Berger pushed me to meet his daughter quickly, within maybe the first three weeks of us dating. I was excited and eager to meet her, but it just felt . . . rushed. But I wasn't the parent and he was, so who was I to make the call about when his child should meet his girlfriend? Against my gut, I went along with his plans because, again, I was thinking, *When you know, you know*. Berger also said "I love you" early on, maybe a month after we met, and though I knew I was well on my *way* to falling in love with him, I wasn't quite ready to say those three little words. But once again—I pushed that pesky gut feeling down as far as it would go and allowed myself to get swept along in the waves of his love and enthusiasm and complete willingness to jump into this relationship with both feet.

But slowly, those great big, rapidly moving waves started to erode the perfect picture I thought we were painting. I suffered from intense anxiety and trust issues, and I was attempting to build a solid relationship on a rocky foundation of dishonesty. Because of the lie Berger told me so early on, I began to struggle with anxiety again, and my gut never quite felt at peace. I couldn't put my finger on it, but something just felt—*off*. And even though Berger had promised me from the beginning that he would be patient with me given the fact that he was the one who had broken the trust, he quickly grew frustrated with my fears and hesitations about the relationship. And I did start to wonder if my anxious mind was just playing tricks on me since, despite our early troubles, he had been the model-perfect boyfriend ever since and I had absolutely no clear reason not to trust him. Was I letting my endless *what if*s destroy my *what is*?

One of my lifelong friends put it so perfectly when we were discussing my concerns about the relationship over lunch one day: "Mandy, I know you tend to be an anxious person, but I also know that if your gut is reacting *this* strongly . . . there's something going on to cause it. Your gut is never wrong."

I didn't have the answers about why I felt the way I did, and I may never know exactly what was causing my gut to feel so unsettled, but what happened next affirmed that the things I was feeling were right on target. Berger and his daughter and I were hanging out one night when, out of nowhere, she blurted out, "Daddy has another girlfriend!" The room went completely silent as I tried to make sense of her statement. Granted, children sometimes say wild and off-the-wall things, but she tended to be pretty serious and incredibly honest and forthcoming for such a little person, so it was hard to imagine she just pulled those words out of thin air. Something was going on that gave her the impression that Berger was involved with another woman besides me. Hurt and confused, I looked at Berger. He wouldn't quite meet my eyes. He rambled and fumbled his way through some sort of explanation, one that didn't ring true to me at all. I felt crushed. I soon came up with a reason to leave, and as I drove home that night, I knew in my heart the relationship was over. I felt embarrassed—ashamed even—that I had fallen head over heels in love with someone who was most likely being unfaithful to me in one way or another. If not physically, then certainly emotionally. I had gone against my gut so many times in the relationship, I couldn't help but feel I could have spared myself worlds of pain had I just listened to my own instincts and years of relationship experience and kept my eyes wide open to what was happening rather than the picture I wanted to see.

Sure enough, about a week after the incident with his daughter, Berger broke up with me in that five-minute-long phone call. The end of the relationship, to him, didn't even warrant a face-to-face conversation. It was hard to feel like anything that had happened between us was real. And it was hard not to blame myself for ending up on the receiving end of such a heartbreaking dismissal. I could have avoided all this had I not been so stuck in the *what if* that I was blinded to the *what is* that was happening right in front of my face. *What if I let this really great guy go for making one mistake and I miss out on my chance for true love?* That question had haunted me in the first couple of weeks of our relationship. And it's a reckoning that single women have to make time and time again as society and our families and friends and social media and pop culture and basically everyone on earth tries to convince us that every man we meet is our last chance at happiness. The weight of everyone else's fears and expectations and dreams for us and their opinions and ideas of what our lives "should" look like can sink us if we're not careful. It can certainly cause us to make wrong choices and to settle or compromise when it comes to love. That's why it's so important to listen to our gut and follow our God-given intuition, even when it doesn't make sense and even when we have nothing whatsoever to go on except our instincts.

Sometimes *what if*s can destroy us. And other times they save us. It all comes down to what your *what if* is rooted in. If it's rooted in fear—for example, *What if I never find another man to love me and this guy is my last chance at happiness?*—it's leading you *away* from yourself and the truth. But if it's rooted in facts—*What if this guy lying to me is indicative of a bigger issue and he's not a safe person I can trust my heart with?*—it's leading you *toward* yourself and your higher truth. Most of the *what if*s in my life are fear-based, so I know to dismiss them and look at what's really happening instead of what I'm afraid might happen. But sometimes, like in the case of Berger, my *what if*s are based on facts and life experience and female intuition, and I should heed them and look at what is happening instead of what I want to happen. It's a tricky thing, navigating the *what if* and the *what is*. And it can cause no small amount of heartache and pain when we act out of fear and ignore the facts.

The overwhelming anxiety I had felt throughout the course of the relationship with Berger, followed by our ensuing breakup, left me in a mess.

About a week after we broke up, I lay down to go to sleep one night and I just . . . couldn't. I've never been the world's greatest sleeper, but I can usually fall asleep fairly easily, even if I wake up a lot throughout the course of the night. But that night, I lay there staring at the ceiling like a hoot owl all night. I felt nervous, I felt sad, I felt edgy. I couldn't stop going over and over the relationship in my mind, wondering how I could have been so wrong about what I thought was the great love of my life. I felt lousy the next day, but I could handle one night of missed sleep.

But then the next night, the same thing happened. Hoot owl, part two. I didn't sleep one wink that night.

By the third night, I was a bundle of nerves and felt anxious even trying to lie down and go to sleep because the *what if*s were plaguing me: *What if I have something wrong with me that's stopping me from sleeping? What if I never sleep again? What if I die from lack of sleep?!* (All anxiety-driven and fear-based *what if*s, of course.)

That was the start of seven days of awful, torturous, debilitating insomnia. Seven whole days and nights without one wink of sleep. When I say I didn't fall asleep for even five minutes in those seven days, that is not an exaggeration. Suffice it to say, as the days went on, I became less like a hoot owl and more like a cat on a hot tin roof. I was a basket case. When you are already suffering from emotional trauma and then you add to that the physical trauma of not being able to sleep . . . the result is disastrous. I was a zombie, but not a slow-moving, lethargic zombie like you see on *The Walking Dead*. I was riding the waves of near-constant panic attacks, so I was like a zombie on crack. The result was not cute. The anxiety and exhaustion and heartbreak had turned me into someone I hardly recognized.

I met with my doctor, who tried several different combinations of medications to try to help me find my way back to sleep. Since I hate taking medication, that trial-and-error process was pretty awful in and of itself. But I was desperate for sleep and willing to try anything. I gave essential oils a go. I meditated and did relaxation exercises and begged God to help me fall asleep. But it wasn't until I just let go and surrendered control that I finally managed to drift off for the first time in over a week. I let go of the breakup, I let go of the idea that I had somehow failed by not being able to make the relationship work, I let go of the idea that I could force myself to fall asleep . . . I finally threw up my hands and *let go*.

And in that moment of surrender, I was finally able to rest. And it was good.

When I fell asleep for the first time in seven days, in a big cozy chair at my parents' house, it felt holy. Sleep is holy. It was only for a couple of hours, but when I woke up, I was crying tears of joy that my body had finally let me rest. You have to rest in order to heal. And I needed desperately to heal.

What got me through the day—and the long nights— during that rock-bottom week was my family. When I couldn't sleep, my parents would sit with me and rub my back or pray for me or just sit quietly so I didn't feel alone. A couple of times, they crawled into the bed with me in solidarity. I was hanging on for dear life, and they gave me the strength I needed to hold on a little longer, reminding me that soon the night would end and the light would break once again. Reminding me, like they always did and like I do for them now, to keep turning toward the sun. It's such a beautiful full-circle relationship, the one between my parents and me. They were there for me in my worst times, and now I get to return the favor for them. Kind of like sunflowers and how, when they can't find the sun, they turn toward each other for warmth and strength. That's my relationship with my mom and dad. They're my sunflowers, and I am theirs. And I'm so grateful for it.

Slowly, the panic attacks subsided. Not all at once, but a little at a time. And gradually, I retrained my body to sleep. Not an entire night through at first, but a few hours at a time until I was back to a regular sleep schedule. Progress often comes in tiny steps forward rather than in leaps and bounds. And that's okay. It's important to recognize and celebrate your progress, no matter how slight. After all, Rome wasn't built in a day, as they say. And neither was a life rebuilt in a day.

The nights during that week or so seemed so very long . . . but eventually, they did end, and eventually, the light did break. And on the other side, therapy was there to bring me the rest of the way home. I found a new therapist who would go on to help me learn more about myself than all of my previous therapists over the years combined.

One of the things she taught me was that people with generalized anxiety disorder—which is what I suffer from—have a tendency to subconsciously use anxiety as a safe haven instead of confronting their grief. It seems crazy to hear that, because who would actively *choose* anxiety? But sometimes the *what if* feels safer than the reality of *what is*. My mind wasn't ready to deal with what was actually happening—the devastating breakup—so I chose instead to camp out in the known safety of anxiety for a while. After all, who knew anxiety better than me? When I look back at it now, I can see that the week of anxiety and intense insomnia and panic attacks following my breakup actually spared me from the pain of having to grieve the loss of the man I loved. The *what if* strangely gave my mind and body and emotions a momentary reprieve because I was too focused on getting through the day to focus on the *what is*—my broken heart. That brings me to something else my therapist said to me that forever changed the way I viewed my anxiety. She said, "Panic and anxiety aren't your body trying to destroy you, they're your body trying to *protect* you." *Whoa.* Game changer right there. Is it possible that what has so often felt like the cause of my rock bottom (my anxiety) has been the thing that got me through the day? And is it possible that sometimes, every once in a while, the *what if* is our salvation and our safety net when the *what is* is too big and painful and scary for our minds and hearts and bodies to comprehend?

That's not to say I'm ready to roll out the welcome wagon for my anxiety and tell it to sit down and stay awhile. I'm still in therapy and working every day to manage my anxiety instead of allowing it to manage me. I'll write more about that a little later. But for now . . . I am learning to trust my body a little more. And to trust myself a little more. And to trust the process a little more. And even to trust that I'm not weak because I suffer from anxiety; instead, I'm strong because I suffer from anxiety but I keep right on fighting. I'm not a failure because I took a chance on love and lost; I'm brave because I was willing to get off the bench and take that chance in the first place. I've come around to the realization that my anxiety, as much as I hate it, can sometimes be a blessing instead of a burden. Because, had it not been for that breakup and the resulting rock bottom I experienced, I wouldn't have aggressively sought the help that I did. And I wouldn't have become nearly as strong as I have, and I wouldn't have even come close to being able to handle everything life would throw at me in the years that followed. Turns out, I had to lose love to find the help I needed and my own inner strength. And I'm okay with that trade-off.

My singleness has been the best training ground for letting go of *what if* and embracing *what is* . . . because it's one of the greatest *what if*s of my life. It's a master class in letting go and surrendering control. I can try online dating, I can put myself out there, I can go on dates, I can even fall in love, but I can't force any of those efforts to turn into love or to last even if they do. And the truth is, we can't do that with anything in our lives. So we have to find a place of acceptance with doing all we can do and knowing that it is enough. Easier said than done, I know. But everything in life that really matters is easier said than done.

So, yes, do everything in your power that you can do to prepare for every situation—whether it be as serious as seeking out a good therapist or as simple as going out on a date. In every scenario you face, be prepared. Be ready. Show up to the battle. But once you've done all you can do, let it go. Know that you've done everything you possibly can, and now it's in God's hands. We are ultimately not in control of what happens or when it happens. But we are very much in control of our reactions and responses. And we can choose peace. We can choose calm. We can choose to trust that the God who started a good work in us will be faithful to complete it (Phil. 1:6).

Maybe the day will come when I feel differently, but for now, I will say this: Picking myself up after the end of that relationship and finding a way to walk away with absolutely zero closure was one of the hardest things I ever did. And I most definitely stumbled more than a little on my way out the door. But it was also one of the best things I ever did because, as it turned out, losing what I thought was great love . . . helped me find myself. New layers of myself. A new strength and confidence and sense of self-love I didn't have before that. And I'm forever grateful to him, and to the situation, for teaching me that walking away from one thing means walking toward everything else.

We always fear that void of walking away from *what if* and into the unknown of *what is*, but I'm here to tell you that on the other side is the rest of your life. So get up, brush yourself off, and start walking, brave, beautiful one. Stumble if you must, but don't stop and don't look back. Your future self is waiting, and she's cheering you on, and she's so very proud of you. And so am I.

6

Planting My Own Garden and Decorating My Own Soul

Despite the things I gained from going through such a painful breakup, I had also lost pieces of myself to my relationship with Berger. When I found myself on the other side of it, I was desperate to reclaim those pieces. I was slowly getting my life back on track and sleeping through the night again, but I had forgotten how to be okay with standing alone. I had forgotten that I determined my worth, not any man or anyone else (other than God). I had forgotten, like an old poem says, how to plant my own garden and decorate my own soul. I was determined to remember how, in a very literal way. I felt like I needed to create something and watch something be birthed from the difficult season I had just come through. I wanted to dig my fingers into the dirt and plant things and watch new life spring up from the desolation of my still-fractured heart. I decided to grow my own little garden on the balcony of my apartment, and I recruited my dad to help me. After a day of scouting out garden centers, I had the makings of my mini-garden: a tomato plant, a bell pepper plant, and sunflower seeds (of course). And with each little seed my dad and I planted that day, I whispered a fervent prayer that someday soon they would sprout, bringing beauty and hope and light with them. It felt almost symbolic to me. If I could get these plants to grow, then surely I could resurrect my own independence and confidence and sense of self-worth.

Over the coming weeks as I diligently watered my little plants and watched every day for new signs of life, tending my balcony garden helped me work through my grief and heartbreak and resulting anxiety. There's something very visceral and restorative about getting your hands dirty to create something new that wasn't there before. And as I worked, God continued to place a Scripture on my heart. He seemed to, time and again, keep bringing me back to this point:

> Listen carefully: Unless a grain of wheat is buried in the ground, dead to the world, it is never any more than a grain of wheat. But if it is buried, it sprouts and reproduces itself many times over. In the same way, anyone who holds on to life just as it is destroys that life. But if you let it go, reckless in your love, you'll have it forever, real and eternal. (John 12:24–25)

One day I had lunch with Laura, one of my dearest friends, and she shared with me that she, too, had recently felt led to Scriptures about seeds and growth and planting and fruit and letting go and letting things die. She was speaking at a retreat that weekend where that was the theme! And I didn't believe in coincidences.

Over the course of the year and a half prior to meeting Berger, I had been through several disappointing relationships or "almost" relationships. They all culminated in the biggest heartbreak of all—my relationship with Berger beginning with such hope and ending with such hurt. This was the man I thought I was going to marry. And, ultimately, he didn't choose me. He chose to walk away instead.

I know this feeling of not being chosen is a struggle for lots of people, not just me. I'm sure you can relate. Especially my fellow single women! So, I then felt led to look up Scriptures about being "chosen by God," and He pointed me to this one. Once again, the theme is of being planted (buried) so you can bear fruit:

> You have not chosen Me, but I have chosen you and I have appointed and placed and purposefully planted you, so that you would go and bear fruit and keep on bearing, and that your fruit will remain and be lasting, so that whatever you ask of the Father in My name [as My representative] He may give to you. (John 15:16 AMP)

I was still trying to make sense of all of it, all these things God was laying on my heart, but as I gazed upon my little sprouts one lovely spring day, it hit me that a few days earlier those sprouts were seeds, tossed into dirt and buried on a wing and a prayer that something good would come of them.

Buried in darkness and then forgotten. To the outside eye, that pot of dirt looked lifeless, hopeless, even a little sad. But the darkness and the dirt were only the beginning of the story for those seeds . . . not the end.

I had been guilty of never truly letting go of relationships, never letting them die. This was evidenced by how long I let my most significant ex, John (aka Mr. E, whom some of you may remember from my previous books), linger around—for over a decade. I even struggled to move on from short-lived relationships because I all-too-often existed in that fearful space of *What if this was my last chance at love and happiness?*

I also frequently go back and try to resurrect long-dead relationships. (Who else is with me in this unfortunate habit?) Another danger of living in the *what if*? You tend to remember only the best parts of relationships and none of the bad. You look at exes through the rose-colored glasses of what could have been instead of the realistic lens of what actually *was*.

I had decided, no more. Something about lovingly tending to my balcony garden was teaching me how to lovingly tend to my own heart. It was time to stop camping out in the safe *what if* of former love and live fully in the glorious unknown of the *what is*. And in what was still to come! It was time to let the past die and to let every old relationship and connection go. Even to let my hopes for marriage go, knowing that if it was something God wanted for me (and I believed it was), the only way to bring it to life was to let it die, once and for all.

The only way to gain your life is by losing it. The first will be last. Die in order to live. Let go to hold on. Release *what if* and embrace *what is*. It's all completely backwards to what the world teaches, but nobody ever accused Jesus of being a conformist. And that's one of the many reasons why I love Him so.

And that's also why I encourage those of you who feel like you've been buried to keep turning toward the sun and keep reaching for the light. Let the past things go and look up at your great big, beautiful present. Because your time to bloom is coming.

How do I know this? Because just a couple of weeks after I buried my little seeds in dirt, they began to spring. First it was the tomatoes, then the peppers . . . and soon, I hoped, the sunflowers.

You know what the whole process of my little balcony garden represented to me? Hope. This is what happens when you let go of *what if*, embrace *what is*, and turn toward the sun. You grow and you change and eventually . . . you bloom. It might take longer than you hoped. It might not happen the way you planned. But given enough time and enough belief in yourself and enough refusal to give up, you will always, always find your way out of the dirt and into the light.

I threw a handful of seeds into a few pots of dirt when I desperately needed to see evidence that darkness never gets the last word.

These little plants and I . . . we spent months stubbornly reaching for the light together.

My tomatoes and peppers had already started rising.

And whether my little sunflower bud chose to bloom where it had been planted or not . . .

I did.

I chose to let the dirt do the work. I chose to let go of *what if* and embrace *what is*. I learned to appreciate the sunny days and the rainy nights. I chose to pull up the weeds that were choking my growth.

I chose to turn toward the sun.

I chose growth. Because growth might be painful and change might be painful, but nothing is as painful as staying stuck somewhere you don't belong.

One day, a couple of months later when I was in Charleston, South Carolina, on vacation with my family, I received the most unexpected picture from my housemate.

My sweet little sunflower had *bloomed*! There it was, like a great big ball of sunshine, waving joyfully in the breeze.

My plant choosing to bloom the minute I went out of town felt very symbolic. Growth doesn't often happen when we're sitting there watching and waiting for it. It happens when we do our part, then let it go.

By the time I got home from the beach and raced out to the balcony to check on my garden, my sunflower plant had two blooms instead of one. Those stubborn little sunflowers would go on to stretch high into the sky, reaching boldly for the sun and bringing a smile to my face every time I saw them.

Watching my little sunflower sprouts grow and change as I myself was growing and changing was such a beautiful thing. I loved how they were always turned toward the sun. Perhaps sunflowers really do hold the secret of life: Be patient and turn toward the sun.

I learned so many lessons from that little sunflower plant. It taught me to trust that, even in the darkest times, the light never leaves us.

It taught me that sometimes all you can do is all you can do . . . and then let it go.

It taught me that the biggest growth tends to happen when we just let all the many *what if*s of life be and exist wholly and simply in the *what is*.

And it taught me that letting go and moving on look impossible at the beginning, messy in the middle, and absolutely gloriously beautiful at the end.

Plant something. Anything. I dare you. It's healing. It's life-affirming. It's a reminder that sometimes we have to let go of our old life and let new life in. Just like we have to stop ruminating on what could have happened or should have happened and simply make space for what *is* happening. So plant something. Toss some seeds into a pot of dirt, water it, and then let it go. Watch what happens next. And next time you're struggling to let go of the old, remember that the new is just underneath the surface, patiently waiting for us to open our hands and our hearts and make room for it to arrive.

Growth is a beautiful thing.

When you reach the place where you're no longer mad or upset or hurt about the way someone chose to treat you or leave you, and you recognize they were just another piece of the puzzle to get you to where you need to be, you've found grace.

When you reach the place where you're no longer sad or heartbroken that someone chose to leave your life, but you recognize that they did you a huge favor by letting you go, you've found freedom.

And when you reach the place where you're no longer regretful or angry or unforgiving toward yourself for any person you chose to be with or any relationship you didn't leave when you knew you should have . . . but you recognize that you were only human, you were doing the best you could, and God was allowing you to settle because sometimes it takes someone *not* seeing your worth and value for you, like a sunflower reaching for the sun, to finally rise up and see it . . .

You've found *yourself*.

7

What If He's the One?

Avoiding Relationship Mirages

I n the life of every single woman, occasionally a brief, or sometimes extended, hiatus from singledom will occur. This phenomenon is commonly known as a "relationship." Yes, for one brief (or not-so-brief), shining moment, your handsome prince gallops into your life and into your heart on his brilliant white horse, and you just know that all is right with the world and that your happily ever after has officially begun.

Never more than in this moment do single women sell their stock in *what is* and take up residence in *what if. What if he's the one? What if this is the beginning of my love story? What if next year at this time I'm married?!* And so on and so forth until you're perusing the bridal magazine aisle at the supermarket and deciding if you want to take his last name or hyphenate it with your own—all before the second date takes place.

Yes, a new relationship can be wonderful, dreamy, and even magical. But all my colorful and painful and sometimes horrifying and hilarious experiences in dating have taught me that it's sooooooo important to try to keep your senses about you in those early days and proceed with caution until you know the other person is just as committed to you as you are to them and that the *reality* of them matches up to the fantasy you've built up in your mind. Because otherwise, it's really, really easy to mistake faux love for the real deal and get so swept up in all the wonderful *what if*s that you completely lose sight of *what is*. And those *what if*s in the early stages of a relationship can often conceal what I like to call "relationship mirages."

What is a relationship mirage? I'm glad you asked.

A relationship mirage is a relationship that, from a distance, appears to be everything you could ever want out of a mate, out of love, and out of a relationship, but once you get a little closer and dig a little deeper, you see that everything you thought to be true isn't. Much like the shimmering water of a mirage in the desert, a relationship mirage looks beautiful, wonderful, refreshing, and life-giving from afar, but up close it's dry, disappointing, soul-sucking, and fake. A relationship mirage is the ultimate *what if* because it tricks you into believing one thing is really another, and it makes you question whether you can trust yourself or your judgment. Is your head wrong, or is your heart wrong? Trying to distinguish the *what if* from the *what is* in those early, heady days of a relationship can be downright impossible, so I want to dig deep into the shadows and march out into the light a few typical relationship mirages to look out for. Because when you've found yourself in the middle of a proverbial dating desert for years on end like I have, sometimes water from the hose can start to look like a tall, delicious glass of sparkling Perrier.

Relationship Mirage #1: The Frog in Prince Charming's Clothing

This relationship mirage is probably the most common and was the situation I found myself in with Berger. A Frog in Prince Charming's Clothing (or a Prince Charming Imposter) looks the part, acts the part, talks the part . . . but doesn't walk the part. This guy falls madly in love with you in record time, calls you the love of his life, and sweeps you completely off your feet (and out of one of your glass slippers), only to turn right around the next day and forget what you look like so he has to try your lost shoe on every girl in the kingdom to find you again. In other words, he's along for the ride as long as everything is seemingly "perfect," but the minute things get real or you show a flaw or something goes a little bit awry in the relationship . . . he'll be gone faster than you can say "bibbidi-bobbidi-boo." The Prince Charming Imposter looks great on paper, but in life—it's a different story. While, on the surface, he appears to be everything you've dreamed of and waited on and hoped for, when you dig an inch deeper, you discover that all that glitters isn't anywhere near gold. He tends to be a serial dater, meaning that while he's your number one, to him, you're just another number in a very long line. And eventually, if you hang around long enough, you will find yourself on the other end of a Post-it-note, text-message, or five-minute-phone-call breakup. Because the only thing this froggy bachelor does faster than fall *in* love . . . is fall out of it.

The Prince Charming Imposter will leave you with a whole lot of *what if*s: *What if the problem is me? What if I just have too many trust issues to believe that someone could really be so wonderful? What if I just move at his pace and ignore my own gut instincts?* But here's the cold, hard *what is* of a Frog in Prince Charming's Clothing: The horse he's riding is on loan, the castle he lives in is really a house of cards, and the words he's been whispering in your ear are from someone else's script. Remember, ladies, here's one *what if* you can always count on with a Prince Charming Imposter: If he seems too good to be true . . . he almost always is.

Relationship Mirage #2: Negging Ned

I've dated guys who have openly rolled their eyes at what I do. I've met guys online who have googled me, seen that I write about single life and inevitably my relationships, and felt so threatened by it, they thought they needed to crack jokes about it or scoff at my blog name or my online presence in order to make themselves feel bigger. I once dated a guy I was actually quite crazy about, until he sat me down on the couch one day and looked me in my eyes and said, "I'm not enough for you. You need someone more important than me." This was a great and very creative way of blaming me for the fact that he either just wasn't that into me or wasn't willing to rise up and be the man I needed him to be.

These guys I'm describing might be different people, but you can call them all by the same name: Negging Ned.

You might be wondering what *negging* is. I get it. I hadn't heard this term myself until a girlfriend of mine defined it for me a few years ago. And as soon as she did, all the pieces clicked. "I've totally dated that guy!" We've all dated that guy, because Negging Ned is everywhere. "Negging is an act of emotional manipulation whereby a person makes a deliberate backhanded compliment or otherwise flirtatious remark to another person to undermine their confidence and increase their need of the manipulator's approval."[1] They may do this to make themselves feel more secure or even so they can end a relationship in a way that lets them off the hook and places the blame for the breakup solely on the other person. So, in other words, they use pointed and passive-aggressive humor to make not-so-subtle digs at you, but the digs come wrapped in a compliment, so that makes it almost impossible to get mad at them.

Negging Ned is kind of like that kid on the playground back in elementary school who pushed you down and pulled your pigtails, and everyone told you it was because he liked you. "We always tease the ones we love!" How could we not grow up to fall for Negging Ned when we're taught from an early age that a guy's being mean to us is a benchmark for how he feels about us?

The biggest *what if*s Negging Ned leaves you with: *What if he really* is *doing these things because he likes me? What if I just laugh at his jokes even if they hurt? It's not that big of a deal.* And especially, *What if I just make myself smaller or less intimidating so he doesn't feel so threatened?*

But the *what is* about Negging Ned that you have to come to terms with is this: No matter how much you like him, any man who can't handle any part of you, whether it be your looks or your smarts or your chosen career path, is a man who clearly can't handle *you*. And you should never have to downplay your successes or water down your personality or apologize for the life you've built for yourself because some man needs you to be less than what you are. There are so many men out there who are so secure in who they are, they would never try to make you question everything about yourself. Why settle for anyone who expects you to play small?

I don't know about you, but I'd rather be alone than settle for a Negging Ned. Because when it comes down to it, the right one for us will always celebrate who we are and what we bring to the table. They won't ask us to leave any part of ourselves behind so they feel more adequate. Only the wrong one will do that. So don't shrink yourself or lessen yourself for anyone, for any reason, ever again. As the late, great Toni Morrison said, "I didn't fall in love, I rose in it."[2]

Relationship Mirage #3: Zombie Guy

There's a song by the Cranberries from the '90s called "Zombie," and the chorus goes, "In your head, in your head . . . Zombie, zombie, zombie-ie-ie."

This song describes Relationship Mirage #3 perfectly because Zombie Guy will have you creating in your head an entire relationship that doesn't even exist. If you've read my last book, *Don't Believe the Swipe*, you might recall from the Modern Dating Dictionary that a zombie is someone who ghosts you but "then reanimates long enough to come back into your life, act interested, and get you back on the hook, only to then turn right around and ghost you again" the minute you reciprocate with the slightest bit of interest.[3]

My own personal Zombie Guy still pops up in my inbox every few months. We met a couple of years ago on a dating app, we went out on a handful of dates that I thought went great, then he completely vanished. Just absolutely disappeared off the face of the earth with zero explanation. So after scratching my head in confusion for a few days, I sighed and moved on, assuming he was a ghost. You can imagine my surprise, then, when he slid into my Facebook DMs a few months later with a "Hey! Let's grab coffee!" I responded a bit hesitantly at first, but after going back and forth with the friendly banter a few times, I decided, hey, it's just coffee. What could it hurt? As soon as I responded favorably . . . Zombie Guy was gone without a trace. Again.

Which brings me to just a few weeks ago when he resurrected himself yet again, popping up in my inbox with a chipper greeting like no time had passed at all. Like it wasn't even slightly weird that we hadn't spoken in almost a year, and yet there he was, once again asking me to hang out. This time it was "Let's catch a movie soon!" I don't know why I even bothered to entertain his message this time. Maybe the loneliness of the pandemic made me soft? But I, per usual, responded enthusiastically, and almost as soon as I did, he, per usual, fell off the face of the earth. This time he at least responded to my acceptance of his movie invite with a weird dog gif before he vamoosed. The whole thing was so nonsensical and bizarre, all I could do was shake my head and sing the lyrics of "Zombie" at the top of my lungs as I deleted his message stream and resolved never to respond to him again.

Here are the big *ifs* you have to watch out for with Zombie Guy: *What if he really likes me and he's just scared?*

or *What if I need to make the first move?* And *What if I'm just not making it clear enough that I'm interested?*

But here's the reality of Zombie Guy's *what is*: He is, at the very least, a complete flake and, at the worst, a major player. He is most likely stringing along three or four other women across various social media platforms. He keeps popping back into your inbox and your life just to see if you're still interested, but he's not quite interested enough to pull the trigger once he finds out you are. And he will keep re-animating and doing his same old Zombie song and dance as long as you'll let him. It's up to you to kill the connection and put Zombie Guy to rest once and for all. Because an actual relationship with Zombie Guy is as much of an oxymoron as *The Walking Dead* (and about as unlikely to happen in real life).

Relationship Mirage #4: Justin Case

I've written at length about this final common relationship mirage in all my previous books. You might remember him as my infamous ex of ten years, Mr. E, aka John. Also known as my very own real-life Mr. Big, named after Carrie's on-again, off-again love on *Sex and the City*. This is someone who's never really quite in but never really quite out of your life. Someone who takes your breath and your heart away simultaneously. Someone who doesn't want to lose you yet doesn't make any effort to keep you. Someone who is stingy with his heart and his time but extremely generous with excuses. Someone you've given chance after chance after chance to get right or get left . . . yet you're still there. Someone you know you should walk away from, but you can't quite force yourself to take that first step. Someone you make excuses for when you know you should be showing him the door.

This not-so-rare species of man is our blind spot. Our strongest weakness. Our almost, not-quite love. The biggest *what if* of our lives. Or, as I also like to call him, Justin Case . . . because he wants to keep you around "just in case." I could talk about Justin Case all day long because he is perhaps the most dangerous relationship mirage there is.

Justin Case is a smooth operator. He knows how to push your buttons. He knows how to get under your skin. He knows how to offer just enough of himself to keep you hooked, sometimes for months and even years at a time. He doesn't really want you to stay, but he doesn't want you to go. He never comes out and says yes, but he also doesn't ever say no. No matter how black or white you need the terms of your relationship to be, you are willing to stay in a perpetual state of gray just to keep him around. You quite obligingly allow yourself to take up residence in relationship purgatory because you're not willing to give up the ghost and move on, but you're also not willing to give up the most and sign on for what could be a life of always being second place. And therein lies the crazy, tragic, almost-but-not-quite-magic conundrum of Justin Case.

Justin Case will be perfectly content to keep you around indefinitely *just in case* something "better" never comes along. For whatever reason, somewhere along the way, he started to see you as the "safe" choice, the in-between girl, the backup plan. Not because you are any of those things but because he is incapable of seeing you clearly enough to recognize the diamond he has standing right in front of him. Perhaps his blinders are there out of fear or immaturity or just pure selfishness. Whatever his reasoning, do you really want to spend another second waiting around for him to realize how incredible you are? The truth is, you can only give a person so much time to realize what's standing right in front of them. You can only let a person chase you for so long before you realize that maybe, just maybe, they never intended to catch you at all.

Justin Case's *what if*s are what make him so very dangerous and hard to let go of and move on from: *What if he's the one for me and I just need to be patient and wait for him to realize it?* and *What if I just put my life on hold and wait for him to pick me, love me, be with me?* and *What if the timing is just off? I don't want to miss out on true love because I wasn't willing to wait for it.* Justin Case would be content to let you wait around in the *what if* for the rest of your life.

But here's Justin Case's great big *what is*: He is a man who, when it comes right down to it, has absolutely nothing to offer you except for meaningless words, empty promises, and endless disappointment. The only way I was finally able to purge my life of my own Justin Case was to get really, really honest with myself about who he was (and wasn't), let go of all my many *what if*s where he was concerned, and accept *what was*. And, ultimately, while he was one of those fun tunes to hum along to for a while, you can only repeat the chorus of a song for so long before you realize the record is skipping, never moving back but also never moving forward. Justin Case is never going to commit to you or me or anyone because he knows he can *not* commit, and we'll still stick around. He thinks he can dance in and out of our lives forever, even cutting in on other partners when he feels like it, because he knows we'll drop anyone at a moment's notice to let him back into our lives. But guess what? It's completely in your power, at any time, to stop the music. It might take two to tango—but it only takes one to walk away.

I have, at one time or another, mistaken all these relationship mirages for love. And I think that's because I used to think love had to be dramatic and theatrical and fraught with Hollywood moments and *what ifs* and "will they / won't they" questions and grand gestures and endless pining and wondering and longing and melancholy in order to be love.

That's what I learned from loving someone for ten years who conditioned me to believe that love was more of a roller coaster than a respite.

It's funny how you change as you get older and wiser and more mature and more confident in yourself.

All of a sudden, the Frogs in Prince Charming's Clothing, and the Negging Neds, and the Zombie Guys, and the Justin Cases don't look so appealing.

My Prince Charming Imposter exited stage left of my life several years ago now. I no longer have time or patience for Negging Ned. Zombie Guy has finally been laid to rest. And Justin Case? Well, his just-in-case girl realized she's a first-place girl. I know myself and love myself so fiercely now, I no longer have even the slightest desire for all the back and forth and endless angst of relationship mirages. I don't even want flashy and showy and Instagram-tailored love. I don't want Mr. Big at all. I'm ready to find my Aidan. I'm ready for gold and not glitter. I want the real deal.

Because love isn't and shouldn't be about the constant high of drama and intrigue and back and forth. It should be about coming home. About finding a safe place to land.

Steadfast. Simple. Sweet. True. *Real.* I think that's what love, real love, should feel like. Not grand gestures . . . but little moments. Not pushing you down on the playground . . . but picking you up when you fall. Not darting in and out of your life with no intentions of committing to you . . . but sticking around, every day, through the good and the bad. Not constant questions . . . but honest answers.

Not the false bravado and sparkly fantasies of *what if* . . . but the raw and real, imperfect truth of *what is*.

Up close and at a distance . . . that's what happily ever after looks like to me.

8

How to Let Go of Love

'll never let go, Jack. I'll never let go!"[1]

In perhaps the most tear-inducing movie scene of all time, found in the fairy godmother of all chick flicks—the film I saw at the theater six times and own not one but two copies of—Kate Winslet's Rose famously makes a promise to Leonardo DiCaprio's Jack that she'll never let him go. She cried, we cried, the person in the next theater over watching *Men in Black* cried, completely enraptured by the sheer beauty and epic romance of Rose refusing to let go of her beloved. The music crescendos, and the magic of the moment transports you to another time and place, until you feel as if you're floating on the next log (Bed frame? Did we ever really decide what the thing was that Rose was floating on?) over from Jack and Rose, watching this beautiful moment in cinematic history take place. Tears roll down your cheeks, your vision blurs, and you start to gulp and hiccup from the intense emotion, waiting for the star-crossed couple to meet their demise together, giving Romeo and Juliet the boot as most popular, most tragic, most romantic couple ever to land on the silver screen.

Then . . . wait a minute. What's happening? She's sitting up. She's kissing him goodbye. She's . . . could it be? Letting him go?!

Though my lip quivers a bit just thinking about that scene, the symbolism of what happens in the film's climactic finale moment is not lost on me. And while some may argue that she only lets him go physically, the fact is, Rose had to also *emotionally* untie herself from Jack, not only to move on with her life . . . but to save her life. Had she opted to cling to him with the same desperation with which she clung to her life raft (and believe me, if Leonardo DiCaprio were holding my hand, I'd be pretty tempted to stay behind, come what may, myself), that would have been the end of her story too.

Rose didn't get the happy ending she had hoped for, because life had other plans for her. And though Rose and Jack are fictional characters, I feel certain that plenty of people (especially single women) know this feeling and have found themselves in similar predicaments: Cling to the *what if* of a sinking relationship for dear life and risk certain disaster and heartbreak? Or let go and move on to *what is*: an uncertain future without the person they thought would be standing beside them for the rest of their lives?

Rose made the decision to let go. As painful as it might have been to release her lover in order to rescue herself, she was determined not to miss out on everything that was coming by clinging to everything that was already gone. And even though she didn't get her happily ever after with Jack, she did get one. In the closing scene of the movie, when we see the older version of Rose peacefully sleeping, the camera pans to countless photos from her colorful and well-lived life. We see that Rose went on to take risks, have adventures, and live life to the very last drop, even without Jack there beside her. Knowing him made her a better person, introduced her to a side of herself she didn't even know existed, and helped her take her first unsteady, hesitant steps toward becoming the woman she was meant to be. But letting him go was the catalyst for realizing her destiny, fulfilling her dreams, and living up to her true potential. The truth is, romantic partners will come into our lives and, in some cases, shake us to our very core along the way; however, not all are meant to stay.

I've talked about how to let go and move on from love in pretty much every book I've written because it's the number-one request I get for advice from single women around the world. And I think it's a lesson worth revisiting, time and again, because no one has to master the art of letting go and moving on from love more than single women. It's literally the story of our lives. And I use the example of Rose and Jack because (1) who doesn't love a good *Titanic* reference, and (2) it's such a perfect illustration of letting go of *what if* and embracing *what is*. Jack was—according to the movie, at least—the greatest love of Rose's life. But, just as significantly, he was also the biggest *what if* of her life. What if he had lived? What if things had been different? What if they had gotten to get off that boat and live out their lives together? What if Rose just stayed with Jack and let go of her own dreams and plans and *life* so she didn't have to face the great big unknown of a future without him? *WHAT IF, WHAT IF, WHAT IF?!* But Rose chose *what is*: a life without Jack. She chose to live. She chose to go on. She chose to surrender the *what if* and face the heartbreak and the loss and the loneliness and the uncertainty of the *what is* head-on. (Or, in other words, she stood and she dealt.)

And eventually . . . Rose turned toward the sun. And she let go of what had been and embraced what would still be. She had a long, beautiful, and meaningful life. She went on to know love again. She realized her biggest dreams. She held the memory of Jack very close to her heart, but she didn't allow that memory to eclipse her reality.

As we weather the choppy waters we call life, this is a decision we will face time and time again: Do we cling to a relationship that's taking us under out of fear of letting go of the familiar? Or do we open our hand and let it go, realizing that heartbreak and loss and loneliness and uncertainty are all part of discovering our destiny?

Though our lost loves (hopefully) won't be as dramatic as Rose's, the principle remains the same. We have to be willing to let go of all the many *what if*s (what we could have done better or differently, what we could have said to make them stay, what might have happened if we had met them at a different time, under different circumstances . . . the list goes on and on and on) and accept *what is*. And *what is*, in the case of lost love, is that the person doesn't want to be with us anymore. Or they can't be with us anymore for whatever reason. Or they're not meant to be with us anymore. The bottom line is, they're not with us anymore. Their part in our story is through. It happened and it mattered, but now it's done. And part of moving on from a relationship that's done is recognizing and even embracing that lost loves are just another part of our journey. A necessary part. A part that allows us to make room for new love, new experiences, maybe even a new *life*. And while that life might look a little different from the one we were expecting, it's just as meaningful and significant and colorful as the one we were planning, if not more so. But you have to be willing to give up the life and love you thought you were meant to have in order to receive the life and love that are meant for you.

If you're a person of faith, like me, making peace with all the many *what if*s of lost love may be particularly challenging. It's hard sometimes to see God's hand in your love life when it keeps getting hit by one *Titanic*-sized iceberg after another. The abrupt and painful end of a romantic relationship is especially confusing when it was with someone you just knew God handpicked for you. I don't know about you, but there have been times in my life when I have pleaded with God to resurrect dead relationships. To make something work that just wasn't working. To bring someone back into my life He helped remove from my life to begin with. To say yes to my endless requests to give me one more shot at the relationship because I just knew this time would be different. Countless nights were spent on my knees saying countless prayers begging for countless yeses from a God who was thankfully merciful enough to tell me no.

Here's the thing, though: That person who broke up with you and shattered your heart didn't *leave* your life. God moved them. So to turn around and bring someone back into your life when He loved you enough to remove them from your life is just simply not in God's nature. (Please bear in mind that I am referring to friendships and romantic relationships that end naturally. I am in no way referencing people lost to us by death.)

God has never given me a no about a romantic relationship when the situation hasn't eventually been turned around for my good. It just hasn't happened. As I've mentioned in this book and detailed at length in previous books, my on-again, off-again relationship that dragged on for ten long years of my life robbed me of so much . . . well . . . *life*. And God finally taking it away from me once and for all was one of the best things that ever happened to me. It forced me to stop *what if*-ing myself to death and live fully in the *what is*. And in the *what is*, I had to confront my own issues, and even confront myself, to find out what it was about me that made me settle for so little for so long. God not answering my prayers to bring this relationship back to life helped me to become more . . . *me*. He gave me the courage and the strength to let things die that had needed to die for a very long time. Had He given me a yes when I begged for it, I would still be stuck in an endless vicious cycle of pain and disappointment and heartache and *what if*. Or, if I were Rose, I'd still be stuck on that bed frame in the middle of the ocean right now. But mercifully, God's no forced me to let go. Not just to let go of the man I thought I loved but to let go of the parts of me that felt so desperate to hold on to someone for more than a decade who so obviously didn't love me. The end of that relationship was the beginning of everything else, and I am so grateful that God let my prayers about it go "unanswered."

We've already established that I've never been great at "letting go and letting God." I prefer to "hang on tight and not let it out of my sight." (LOL!) But then I think about situations like the one I found myself in way back in my twenties. There was a guy at church I was convinced

I was destined for. I was so very sure he was the one God had for me. (It also didn't help that the guy flat-out told me he was the guy God had picked for me.) But just a few months into our friendship, he abruptly turned cold as ice and walked away without ever really offering any sort of explanation about what had happened or why he had such a sudden change of heart. I was obviously heartbroken and left wondering if there was any order or meaning to things or if everything is arbitrary and random. It was hard for me to understand why God would allow someone to tell me he was my future husband only to then turn around and disappear.

It's taken two decades and lots of hindsight for me to see that if I had been this man's wife . . . that's all I would have ever been. A pretty face on a Christmas card, someone to be seen and not heard, a woman "fit for the kitchen but not for the boardroom." That was the prevailing attitude of the church I was a member of at that time, the same church that guy later became a leader of. I would have never accomplished all the things I have if that relationship had worked out. I would have never become a positive voice for single women—and really all women—around the globe. I would have never found my voice at all. That relationship was one great big *what if* that would have completely brought to a halt the great big *what is* that God had planned for me. And God, in all His infinite wisdom, knew that. So now when a guy flakes or ghosts or breaks my heart in a baffling way, it helps me to look back at the other situation and remember that what is for me will be for me. When God removes something or someone from my path or tells me no or seems slow to answer, it's only because He knows the end before the beginning even happens, and He has a better plan for me than I have for myself.

He does for you too. You can let go. It's safe.

If you're feeling like God has turned His face from you or is ignoring your prayers about a certain relationship, please hold tight to the beautiful knowledge that He hears all, He sees all, He knows all. He isn't ignoring you. He hasn't forgotten you. He loves you too much to give you a yes now that would cost you His best later. And He definitely loves you too much to let you stay stuck in the *what if* when the *what is* is waiting and is so much better.

Recently a girlfriend said something to me about my life that was almost verbatim something my therapist had said a couple of months earlier. (When a message comes to you multiple times from different sources, you might want to pay attention. That's not typically accidental. It's usually divine order.)

What did she say? Well, the gist of it was this:

"Mandy, you have so much faith when it comes to your career. You don't doubt or fear; you just let go and trust God to work it out. And magic happens! Why can't you have that same faith when it comes to love?"

BOOM.

It's so true. I've always surrendered the many, many *what ifs* of my career path to God and trusted Him with it completely, and I've had some of the most ridiculously wonderful and even downright miraculous career opportunities come my way as a result. Not by my hand or my might but by His. And yet . . . and yet . . . when it comes to my personal life, and to romantic relationships, I cling. I stress. I worry. I try to control. And I always end up "crushing the butterfly," as my therapist likes to say. I get so hung up on the *what if*s that I miss out on the *what is* altogether. And I struggle to release my Jack Dawsons, even when it's clear they're deadweight that will do nothing but impede me from the life and love God has for me.

The great irony of this struggle is that my favorite Scripture is Psalm 46:10: "Be still, and know that I am God" (NIV). The New American Standard Bible translates it "Cease striving and know that I am God" or "Let go and know that I am God" (1995).

Maybe it's time for us to get really, really still and to cease striving and just *trust*. Trust Him to bring the people and relationships into our lives that are meant for us and to remove the ones that aren't. And to help us make peace with the ones He removes, knowing that He never, ever takes anything from us without the intention of replacing it with something better. Maybe it's time to just trust Him completely, with the *what if* and the *what is*—of all aspects of our lives, romantic and otherwise.

When you let go, something magical happens. You give God room to work. (You might have seen these words of wisdom floating around on Pinterest. And who wrote them? Me. Why am I so bad at taking my own advice?)

For those of you who, unlike me, are actually good at taking advice, here are a few practical tips for letting go of lost love and giving God room to work:

1. Probably the most important key to moving on, one that is often overlooked or ignored in the attempt to outrun the pain and discomfort of sadness: You must allow yourself to grieve it if you wanna leave it.

If you wanna heal from it, you're gonna have to deal with it—plain and simple. Let yourself feel the loss of *what if* and all the ideas and dreams and plans you had for the relationship. Don't run. Don't hide. Don't try to push away or reject the pain or the loss. Let it in. Let it all the way in. Embrace it. Feel it . . . every last bit of it. It takes feeling to start the healing. And healing is messy. Scream, cry, cuss, throw things if you need to . . . but do something to let yourself feel the loss. Because that loss is the key to your transformation. There's a quote from *Eat, Pray, Love* by Elizabeth Gilbert that I think sums up this process perfectly: "Someday you're gonna look back on this moment of your life as such a sweet time of grieving. You'll see that you were in mourning and your heart was broken, but your life was changing."[2]

The brokenness I experienced from my ten-year, on-off relationship coming to an end has led to so much beauty and growth and change in my life. It pushed me to finally seek help for the overwhelming sense of lack I had felt for years. It made me realize how strong I really am. It inspired multiple books! It completely upended and destroyed and refined and rebuilt me. In hindsight, I can see now that it was one of the best things that has ever happened to me. Loss and heartbreak can teach you so much, if you'll let them. Getting down to nothing has a magical way of reminding you that you are *everything*.

Bottom line: You can't move past something until you walk right up to it and move through it. You must confront your hurt and your loss and your sadness,

sit down with them, look them dead in the eye, allow
yourself to feel every emotion without judgment . . .
and before long, you won't have to worry about letting
go of your heartbreak because it will have let go of you.

2. Purge constant reminders from your living environ-
ment. You can't truly move on and get excited about
new opportunities for love that life has in store if
you're still physically living in a time capsule of
everything that has come before. You don't have to
hold a "cleansing ceremony" and burn all his belong-
ings à la the infamous *Friends* episode circa 1995,
but if you're still sleeping in his favorite sweatshirt
and spraying yourself with his cologne every night—
you're still planted firmly in the *what if*, and it's time
to come back to the *what is*.

Pack up all the pictures, clothes, CDs, stuffed
teddy bears, anything that keeps you tied to his
memory, and store them away somewhere safe. I
recommend not throwing them away because there
might come a day when these tokens elicit smiles
instead of sadness, but I would also steer clear of a
big, dramatic "return the things" meeting with him,
also known as "an excuse to see him one last time."
If you tuck everything away in a safe place, you can
always go back later when you're feeling stronger
and decide what to do with it without having to
stare at it on a daily basis. There really is something
to the whole "out of sight, out of mind" theory.

3. Call your closest friends and tell them to circle the
wagons. When your soul is in need of a little chicken

soup, there is nothing more comforting than the presence of your soul sisters. Go dancing, go see a movie (a comedy—not a sappy chick flick!), get a pedicure, consume large amounts of chocolate, and let the warm sunshine of friendship dry your tears.

Chances are, if you've been wrapped up in a serious relationship for the past several months or years, you might have been neglecting your girl time anyway, so there's no time like the present to reestablish those bonds of sisterhood! After all, as Carrie Bradshaw once said, "No matter who broke your heart, or how long it takes to heal, you'll never get through it without your friends."[3]

4. Get reacquainted with *you*. What have you been putting on the back burner while you've been fanning the flames of love? Get back in touch with your passions, your dreams, your goals. Start a new hobby. Visit a new church. Pursue a new interest. Try yoga. Join a book club. Volunteer. Do something to contribute to the greater good of the world and the greater good of your soul, and before you know it—you'll be smiling again. Focus all the energy you've been focusing on him on something *you're* passionate about. Amazing, unbelievably good things start to happen when you follow your gut, your truth, your passions, your heart.

5. Finally, remember this:

   You will get over him. You will. You think you won't, but you will.

   It might be the worst heartbreak you've ever experienced. It might be the thing that brought you to your knees. It might have caused you to lose sleep, lose sanity, lose time, or lose your faith in yourself watching them walk away.

But there will come a day when you will wake up and it won't hurt quite as badly. And then the next day . . . it will hurt a little less.

And then one day it won't hurt at all.

And then one day, not long after that, you'll stop crying that they're gone . . . and you'll breathe a sigh of relief that they left.

Because anyone, absolutely anyone, who could have your wild, imperfect, beautifully-stronger-at-the-broken-places self in their life and not do anything and everything in their power to hold tight to your love is not someone who deserves it.

I am learning to trust endings now, even when I don't understand them. Sometimes God allows our hearts to be broken *then* to protect our now. He brings about our *what is* by removing the *what ifs*. Even if He has to remove them against our will. His will, not ours, be done.

Every once in a while, we are given a glimpse behind the curtain at His perfect plan, and it helps us see that the thing that hurt us and broke us, and maybe even almost killed us, happened to prevent the bigger hurt and bigger brokenness and certain destruction waiting for us a little farther down the road.

Recently, a sweet friend said something so beautiful to me: "There's a strength in showing up despite the hurt." For a long time, I was showing up to my life, despite the hurt of all the *what ifs* and *The Ends* and the lost loves that never became true loves over the past few years. But then, slowly, I started showing up and barely thinking about the hurt. And then, pretty soon, I was just showing up because I was excited to show up, without even a twinge of hurt. I guess that's what healing looks like. It's also what living fully in *what is* looks like. Today, I can honestly look back on the last few years and lost loves with nothing but gratitude because every single person who came into my life and every single person who left it played a role in molding me into a stronger, better woman than I would have been otherwise. And I am thankful.

"It doesn't make sense. That's why I trust it," Rose said in *Titanic* about getting off the boat with Jack. The same could be said for God's plan. We might not understand His plans for our romantic future . . . but He does. And we can trust Him, even when His answers aren't what we hoped for. Because His yeses might be blessings . . . but His nos are great big, beautiful grace, leaving great big, beautiful space to trust Him even more and to welcome the things and people into our lives and hearts that *are* meant for us. He nos . . . because He knows.

You can let go. You can trust Him. You can trust *The End*.

Because after every *The End* comes another opportunity to begin again.

Nothing and no one that were meant to be yours ever get away.

9

To the Man I Thought Was "the One"

To the Man I Thought Was "the One," or My "Almost, Not-Quite Love":

This is the last time I will ever write about you. I've given you pages, chapters, books of my life . . . but it's time for me to write a new story. One without you in it. I'm finally ready to do that now. But to start a new chapter, you must first close the old one. And to fully embrace *what is*, you must first release *what if*.

For years, I asked God to bring closure to this relationship with you . . . or, if not closure, at least a little clarity about what it all meant. This on-again, off-again, never-quite-together, never-quite-apart, yes-and-no, back-and-forth, *what-if* relationship. What was your greater purpose in my life, if not to be my forever love? It just didn't make sense to me. But then again, I guess that's what faith is all about: trusting God and moving forward anyway, even when it doesn't make sense. And that's what I did. For ten long years. I thought I knew the ending. I thought I knew God's plan.

But I was wrong.

Instead of walking down an aisle to you, I walked down a long, often heartbreaking path with you. One that tested me, challenged me, tried me, and always, always pushed me closer to God. I spent years trying to get closer to you, but God in His infinite wisdom knew that what I really needed was more of Him. And that's what this relationship represents to me. It's what it will always represent to me: A giant question mark in my life that pushed me ever closer to the One who is the answer . . . the One who is the beginning and the end . . . the One who loves me enough to heal any wounds left by someone who could never quite love me enough. The biggest *what if* of my life that helped me come to know the heart of the One who was and is and is still to come deeper than I might ever have known Him otherwise. It wasn't until I was willing to finally surrender you 100 percent to God that He was able to show me the reason for you. The bigger picture. The purpose of every tear, every disappointment, every one of the ten long years I spent waiting for you to love me back.

You see, my almost, not-quite love . . . the number ten in the Bible represents completeness. And God showed me in that tenth year of you and me that it would be the year we would finally be complete, in one way or another. And over the course of that tenth year, the meaning of our relationship came completely into focus: You weren't the one I was meant to share my life with. You never were. You were the one who was there to teach me how to share my life, my whole life, my whole heart and soul, with God. Completely and unequivocally, holding nothing back.

"Pursue Me the way you want a man to pursue you, Mandy," God had whispered into my heart during one of our many quiet times.

You see, my almost, not-quite love . . . there came a day when my eyes were opened to the fact that the way you had been with me for all those years—wishy-washy, lukewarm, undecided, half-in, half-out—was the way I had been with God. Never fully committed. On fire one day and ice-cold the next. Unwilling to invest my full self into the relationship. How it must have broken His heart.

The same way you broke mine, over and over again.

Then, on a summer day of that tenth year, you looked me in the eyes and told me once and for all:

"I don't love you."

You could have told me that at any point during those ten long years . . . but you didn't. And you know what? I'm glad you didn't. Because the farther you pulled away from me . . . the closer you pushed me to God. Oh, the conversations I had with Jesus that started off about you but turned into intimate, precious, communion with Him about every topic under the sun! I spoke, He listened. He spoke, I listened. So many heartfelt, transparent, real, raw, candid moments I shared with my precious Jesus . . . all because I was driven to my knees in prayer about you and for you.

So you see, my almost, not-quite love . . . I don't regret you. How could I? We had some beautiful moments over the years, yes, but the moments I had with God as a result of our not-so-beautiful moments are ones I will cherish forever.

No, I don't regret you. You taught me how to embrace the beautiful uncertainty of my life and to trust that nothing, absolutely nothing bad can happen to me that God can't find a way to turn for good.

You taught me that giving one's heart away is always brave, regardless of whether or not the other person chooses to accept it.

You taught me how to turn toward the sun and to turn toward the Son. Because of you, I learned that even the darkest night of my soul is no match for the light.

You taught me how to love myself better. You taught me how to love other people better. And most of all, you taught me how to love *God* better.

Without you, I might not be the woman I am today.

And I can finally say, with my whole, entire heart . . .

It is finished.

Thank you.
Mandy

10

Turning Toward the Son

've talked about my faith pretty significantly in previous chapters, so I thought it was time to just give it its own chapter. Because what is faith if not the ultimate *what if*?

For my entire life, I've identified as a Christian. I went to church sporadically as a child and went through the whole process of getting saved and then baptized when I was around ten or eleven. But it wasn't until I was twenty that I really came to know God. I talked about this at length in my second book, *I've Never Been to Vegas, but My Luggage Has*, but for those of you who haven't read that book, allow me to recap.

When I was in college, I joined a church for the first time in my life. And when I say "joined a church," I mean I was *all in*. I got radically saved. And I devoted my life to God in a way that I never had before. I was a member of that church for five years, completely devoted, completely sold out, completely invested in the people and the movement.

My entire life revolved around the church . . . until the day it didn't. The church was a wonderful safe haven for me. It helped me come to know God in a new and deeper way. It brought new friendships into my life. It filled my days and nights with endless activities: Bible studies and youth ministry and conferences and serving. But as I moved up the ladder of leadership and came to see the inner workings of the church, I began to notice what I was too young and naïve to identify at the time but what I now know was extreme legalism and even hypocrisy. Guys and girls weren't allowed to ride together in the same car to church events because we had to "avoid the appearance of evil." We were instructed to throw away entire stacks of CDs and DVDs that were not "honoring to God." The women were harshly reprimanded if we wore spaghetti straps or anything that would "cause the men to stumble." MTV was dubbed "Mucus Television" by my pastor. Not to mention the hate and judgment that were rained down from the pulpit upon various groups of people who happened to be different from us. The church introduced me to God's wrath with nary a word about Jesus's grace. Having an intimate relationship with Jesus Himself was never mentioned to me during my years there. The goal seemed to be less about serving God and more about serving the pastors. Do more, be perfect, don't sin, don't cause anyone else to stumble . . . *or else*.

I never quite measured up to the church's standards of perfection. I had a little too much spirit. I laughed a little too loud. I dared to plan events that included both guys and girls because I knew how innocent and pure our friendships were. I didn't agree that women should be seen and not heard, and I even (gasp!) wore a spaghetti-strap top to an event in sunny California. The straw that broke the camel's back for me was when the staff held a meeting to discuss my V-neck dress without bothering to invite me. I was told I didn't have "discernment in the area of clothing." That opened my eyes to the fact that I was exhausted, my spirit was broken, and the church I once loved and felt so at home in was now causing me more pain than peace.

So after five years at the church, I walked away and I never looked back. And for years afterward, I struggled with how that experience made me feel about myself. The *what if*s I took away from that experience were almost crippling. *What if it wasn't that I just simply wasn't good enough for them? What if I wasn't good enough for God? What if I wasn't holy enough? What if I was bound for hell for daring to stand up for myself and walk away? What if I really didn't have any discernment in the area of clothing?* For a long time, I felt cheap and sinful and wrong for wearing miniskirts and sundresses and normal things that twentysomething girls wear. I struggled to let myself be seen in public in a bathing suit. And the impact that the church's influence had on my dating life was detrimental. They taught us that dating was against God's plan and showed a lack of faith in His ability to bring us a life partner. So I stopped dating for years because I thought I was doing something wrong by wanting to spend time with and get to know guys if we weren't altar-bound. But how could you know if you were destined for marriage if you didn't date? It was all so convoluted and toxic, and it cost me years of formative dating experiences that so many of my now-married counterparts had. I'm honestly still working through some of the trauma and messed-up theology they left me with, and I chalk up my singleness at age forty-two in no small part to the residual negative impact of those teachings on my dating life.

While that experience temporarily broke my spirit, I'm happy to say, by the grace of God, it didn't break me. And thank God all churches don't reflect what that one did. It was extremism and legalism at their worst. But after leaving that church in my midtwenties, I've struggled to feel connected to and truly at home in another church. I have a pattern of starting to get plugged into a church only to get too close to leadership and see things, no matter how slight, that remind me of the church that caused me so much pain; then I pull back before I get hurt like I did before. I think a lot of believers struggle with this feeling. Once bitten, twice shy.

I'm not saying I was perfect or that I didn't do anything wrong during my time at the church. I know I did. I was young and impulsive and still figuring out who I was, and I probably needed correcting at times. (Nor did I expect them to be perfect.) But the way they went about the correcting, and the way they made women—particularly single women—feel about themselves was extremely damaging. We were told we were too vocal. Too flirtatious. Too sexy. Too loose. Too independent. Too rebellious. Too opinionated. We were always too much and never enough.

Even today, as an older and wiser woman, I'm still often caught between "too much and never enough" in my day-to-day life as a writer. I am not your typical Christian author. I never have been. Some people think I'm too "spiritual." Other people think I'm too "worldly." It's impossible to walk a perfect balance between the two that pleases everyone. But I've come to realize this: I'm not your stereotypical Christian author because I'm not your stereotypical Christian.

Especially not when much of modern Christianity seems to have lost its collective mind. Or as writer Laura Robinson recently put it so succinctly on Twitter, "I do not think as a culture we have yet come to grips with the fact that people are leaving organized religion not because they are attracted to vice, but because they are attracted to virtue and the people we keep offering as guides and models to them just don't have [it]."[1] For the moment, I have taken a break from organized religion, not just because of my past negative experiences but because I've searched all around and can't seem to find one that fits the criteria I need—love for and acceptance of *all* humans, not just the ones who are like me. So no, I am not your typical "Christian." But I love Jesus, and I long to serve Him and follow Him and be more like Him. And at the end of the day, that's what really matters.

It's okay if you don't fit into some nice, tidy little Christian mold. In fact, you know who never fit into some nice, tidy little Christian mold? Jesus. You know who rejected the religious to walk with the ragamuffins? Jesus. You know who was more concerned with how you love than who you love? *Jesus.* So yes, the door is open for you too. Regardless of how far outside the "Christian" sphere you might find yourself. It always has been. It always will be.

I don't know about you, but I'm done fighting the battle of too much and never enough. I'm done. I'm just going to be me. And if I'm someone who laughs too loud or loves my imperfect and different friends too fiercely or votes for someone other Christians don't approve of or wears a skirt that's too short or talks about Jesus too much, then you're just gonna have to get over it. (Insert fist-bump emoji here.)

Someone asked me not too long ago what my "biblical worldview" is. Back in my twenties, I probably would have had some really long, impressive response, complete with charts and graphs and biblical annotations to back it up. Today, my biblical worldview is this: I love Jesus, and I love His people. All of His people. It's as simple as that.

That doesn't mean I don't find Him to be incredibly complicated. I do. I don't understand a lot of things about God. A whole lot of things, actually. I especially don't understand some things people do in His name. There are so many *what ifs* I might not ever find answers for—on this side of heaven, at least. I don't believe God causes bad things . . . but why does He allow them? Why does He allow cancer and pandemics and racism and hate and even His own proclaimed people to use His Word as an instrument of hurt and destruction? Why do bad things happen to good people and good things happen to bad people? Why did He welcome mosquitoes onto the ark instead of letting them meet their very timely waterloo?

I don't have all the answers and I never will, and I'm not a Bible scholar and I never will be, but what I do know for sure is that God sent Jesus to bridge the gap between Him and us, and I love and trust Jesus with my whole heart. And although as I get older I seem to have more and more unanswered questions and lingering *what ifs* where my faith is concerned, there are three things I've come to know for sure, or three *what is* certainties we can always count on when it comes to God.

First: You can be 100 percent real with Him. You don't have to approach Him with fancy words or with what I like to call "Christianese." You don't have to be polite. You don't have to be anything other than exactly who and what you are, and you can know beyond a shadow of a doubt that He loves you anyway. Nothing about us is a surprise to God. He knows it all—the good, the bad, the ugly—and He loves us anyway. I dare say He might even love us *because* of our flaws rather than in spite of them. I think a broken, bruised, brutally honest person who falls at His feet with zero pretense or prettiness or politeness is much more beautiful and even beloved to Him than someone who approaches Him from a pedestal of "perfection." Give me imperfection over the pedestal all day long. If you've never gotten angry with God . . . if you've never flailed and screamed and cried and presented Him with your long list of *what if*s and *why*s . . . I'd ask you to consider how authentic your relationship with Him really is. Because a full, real, living, breathing relationship with the Creator of the universe is not all sunshine and daisies and unicorns and puppies, and it's not supposed to be. It should be as real and messy and up and down and wild and unbridled as life itself. God gave us free will so we could come to Him just as we are. He can handle you, just as you are. He wants you, just as you are. He loves you, just as you are. We can . . . and we must . . . get real with God. He can handle it. Wherever you're at in your life, tell Him. If you're hurting, tell Him. If you need Him desperately, tell Him. If you're angry at or mistrustful of Him because it feels like He's not showing up in your life, tell Him. Whatever it is, *tell Him*. He already knows anyway.

Second: Jesus loves you.

Not as you'll be. Not as you want to be or hope to be or plan to be . . . someday.

But just as you are, right now.

Imperfections and all. Mess and all. Going to church or not going to church.

Jesus loves you.

<Full stop.>

I once went looking for quotes about the wholeness and entirety and perfection of God's love, and instead I found a bunch that said things like "God loves you as you are, *but*" (followed by some self-righteous, self-help-y line about how He loves you, *but* He loves you too much to let you stay as you are).

But here's the thing.

His love is unconditional. He knew just what He was doing when He created you. So there are no buts or conditions attached to His love. His love is pure and complete and completely without conditions or stipulations.

It. Is. Finished.

And not up for discussion.

He loves you. Just as you are. In this moment. Without changing a thing. Jesus loves you.

Rest in that today and every day.

And third: Your faith will sometimes waver. This is a fact if you are a believer. There will be seasons on the mountaintop when you feel like God is ordering your every step and seasons when it feels like He has completely turned His face and removed His presence from you. You will have days when you are mad at Him. Days when you question Him. Days when you doubt His very existence. If you're like me, you'll even have days when you scream and flail and turn away and rebel. But here's the really beautiful thing about God. Are you ready?

He can handle it.

He really can.

All of your questions and fears and tantrums and tears. Every last one of them. He's big enough and merciful enough to handle everything you throw at Him and to love you all the way through to the other side of it. Because He's got you. And He's not letting go. Even when you let go of Him. Especially then. I can't explain why sometimes He feels distant. Or why sometimes prayers go unanswered. Or why things happen the way they do. But I know that His grace covers me in all my imperfect humanness . . . and even when you don't feel it, it covers you too.

————

I've been on this wild road trip with God for more than twenty years now, and even though I have more *what if*s now than I did when I started, I am content to keep turning toward the Son and trusting Him to work out the *what is* as we go. Lord knows there have been times when I've strayed off course and taken my own detours and wandered off to go see the world's largest ball of yarn, thereby fully missing the jaw-dropping beauty of the Grand Canyon that He was trying to show me. But I think the beauty of God is that He redeems those ball-of-yarn moments and turns them into Grand Canyon moments. He makes all things beautiful: the *what if* and the *what is*. He makes every part of our story sacred and meaningful: The questions and the answers. The wondering and the wandering. Even the moments we completely veer off-road and settle for less than His best. Yes, looking back I can see how every moment of my life has been full of Him, even when I wasn't seeking after

Him . . . because once He chooses you, you're chosen. And guess what? *He chooses us all.* And it's up to us to choose Him back. So here's to my world's largest ball of yarn and my Grand Canyon moments and to continuing this joyride with God, trusting that every detour, every roadblock, every time I get hopelessly lost is another part of my story and it all matters and it's all beautiful. And even though I haven't yet made it to the Grand Canyon . . . I know we'll get there someday. God and me. (But we're totally stopping for snacks on the way.)

11

No One Is Forever 21

One of the biggest leaps of faith in life has to be learning how to age gracefully. Especially as a single woman "of a certain age."

I've never been married, so I can't speak from that perspective, but I do think it surely has to be easier to face growing older when you have your "'til death do us part" to be there by your side, through all the wrinkles and extra pounds and weird aches and pains and sagging and gray hairs. When you're single and facing down the barrel of middle age, the *what ifs* seem to grow louder than the ticking of your biological clock with each passing year. *What if I never meet someone and get married? What if it's too late for me? What if I'm an old maid? What if I never have children? WHAT IF, WHAT IF, WHAT IF?!*

We have no control over aging, and feeling out of control is incredibly triggering for me. (As it is for anyone with anxiety.) A few years ago when I found myself facing a milestone birthday—forty (*Gulp!*)—the panic and anxiety about growing older began to set in. I didn't feel mature or established or settled enough in my life to be turning forty.

Forty had always loomed sort of big and scary on the horizon. I remember celebrating my twenty-ninth birthday and putting "Come help me celebrate my last year in my twenties!" on the invitation. As though thirty was *so old* (insert eye-roll emoji here). All during my twenty-ninth year, I had major anxiety about trading the two in my age for a three. But then the day arrived . . . the big 3-0 . . . and it wasn't so scary after all. It didn't feel much different than twenty-nine. It helped that my early to midthirties were pretty life-changing for me, in the most amazing ways. I had traded in my full-time job in public relations, complete with its benefits, job security, and 401(k), for a full-time job as a writer, complete with none of the above. And against all odds, I had achieved success! My thirty-third year, I published my first book. My thirty-fourth year, I hit the *New York Times* bestseller list with my second book. I even got to check "Work with Oprah" off my bucket list. I was on a career high and loving life in my thirties. For a while, I forgot all about the impending 4-0.

Then my late thirties arrived, and with them . . . life challenges. Personal, romantic, career, family—I was hit on all sides with great big, life-altering things. And I floundered. I struggled. I faced battles with depression and anxiety. For the greater part of the last three years of my thirties, I felt like I was fighting to keep my head above water. Then thirty-nine was upon me, and the dread I had felt a decade ago about turning thirty started to rear its ugly head again. And as my thirty-ninth year went on, edging me ever closer to the big day, the angst about letting go of my thirties drew to a fever pitch. Lordy, Lordy . . . I wasn't ready to turn forty.

So on one particularly anxious day, rather than sitting around obsessing about my fading youth, I did what any intelligent, self-actualized, mature thirty-nine-year-old woman would do.

I went shopping at Forever 21.

Because, you know . . . there's no better way to forget about your fading youth than to go shopping at a store that celebrates being eternally youthful.

I did my usual perusing of the aisles, grabbed a few things off the racks, including a super cute blouse in size small (I typically wear a small or medium in tops), and headed for the dressing room. Though the blouse slid on with ease, I was disappointed to see that it was a little tight in the arms. *Oh well,* I thought. *On to the next.* Except . . . when I went to take off the blouse, it was stuck. Like, literally wouldn't budge from my body. My body and the shirt were one. After contorting myself into unnatural positions for a good ten minutes, trying to ease the top off so as not to tear it, it got stuck halfway on and halfway off, making it hard for me to breathe. I started to feel a little panicky, claustrophobic even. I was trapped halfway in and halfway out of a blouse that was so fused to my body, it might as well have been a straitjacket. I twisted and turned, bent and snapped, and still the blouse refused to budge. Finally, I was left with no choice but to creep out of the dressing room in my pretzel-like state and ask for assistance from the closest sales associate I could find. She stood there, peering at me from outside my dressing room door, tapping her chin and looking completely confused for a good two to three minutes, contemplating what to do. Eventually, she bent me over and started pulling and tugging and yanking at the shirt. Unfortunately, it budged just enough to make it even harder for me to breathe. This tug-of-war went on and on until I was about to burst into tears, and I started screeching for the associate to just cut it off my body and I would pay for it. She stopped her game of tug-of-war with the top, considered this for a moment, then said, "Let me go get my manager." Thus began another several-minute wait with me standing there in the middle of the dressing room in a strapless bra and a shirt halfway on and halfway off. (Also with me gasping for breath and on the verge of a major anxiety attack.) Finally, the manager appeared with a hesitant smile on her face like she thought I was about to break out of the shirt, Incredible Hulk–style. She, too, commenced with the yanking and tugging of the evil cage of a blouse as people walked by, staring curiously into my wide-open dressing room. Just before I lost consciousness from lack of oxygen, she managed with one final fierce yank to free me from the shirt, but not without leaving my carefully braided hair in a tangled, static electricity–ridden nest that looked like I had just pulled my finger out of a socket.

I darted out of the store as fast as my legs would carry me, my near brush with death by blouse leaving me a changed woman. It took that fiasco for me to realize that while I might still love Forever 21, I was no longer Forever 21. And though I might still visit it from time to time, it was clearly no longer a store that fit my needs. Or my age. Or my style. Because the thing is, no one is "forever" anything. No matter how much we might want to be. Life doesn't come with a pause button and it's not meant to. We're not here to stop, to hesitate, to grow stagnant in any one particular season or place or era of life. We're meant to move, to grow, to change, to let go, to evolve . . . to release the *what ifs* of our past and embrace the *what is* of our present and future. Why? Because it's impossible to turn toward the sun and bloom when you're trying so hard to stay planted in a place—or an age—where you no longer belong. And it's also:

- Painful. Just as my body contortions to try to force a shirt to fit me at Forever 21 hurt my arms and shoulders and ribs and ego, trying to force yourself to stay stuck in a season of life you've already outgrown hurts your heart.
- Constricting. The ill-fitting Forever 21 shirt constricted my lungs and my ability to breathe. Staying in a place where you no longer fit constricts your movement and your ability to grow in the direction your life is calling you.
- Limiting. Clinging to my "Forever 21" mindset stopped me from fully stepping into my sense of style and embracing all the many boutiques out there with fashions that accentuate who I am *now*, today. Clinging to anything you've outgrown will do nothing but hold you back from moving into the next phase of your life, a phase filled with new and better people and situations and places and opportunities (and maybe even better clothes).

It can be hard to admit when it's time to let go and move on. It can be humbling. It can be sad. It can be scary. It can be challenging. Especially when what you're letting go and moving on from is the shiny, sparkly *what if* of your youth and all the dreams and plans and goals you had for yourself and your life that you might not have lived up to. But to become who you are meant to be, you are required to surrender who you used to be. And as uncomfortable and uncertain and anxiety-inducing as it might feel, growing older is a good thing! It means you're still growing . . . into something bigger, something better, something more beautiful and colorful and unique. Something more like yourself. And just because you left a few *what ifs* behind you doesn't mean that the *what is* in front of you can't be really freaking amazing.

As I was recounting my Forever 21 debacle to my therapist a few days later and sharing with her the resolve it left me with to stop clinging to who I had been so I could make space for who I could still be, she told me she was so proud of me and how much I had grown in the time we had been working together. Then she asked what I was most proud of from my thirties. What was my biggest accomplishment? After thinking about it for a moment, I knew it wasn't any of my career achievements, exciting as they might have been, but my willingness to confront myself and my own stuff over the past few years. Because somewhere in the midst of my late thirties, I had simply grown tired of my own nonsense. Which is the first step to change. Real, genuine, lasting change. I had stopped running from my own junk, and I had started confronting it. Unwaveringly. And I was really super proud of that fact. There are people who run from themselves and their issues for their entire lives, and they might appear to be a lot more "together" than I am on the outside, but the truth is, they're crumbling on the inside. And while I might sometimes crumble on the outside, I was getting stronger every single day on the inside. This journey of self-discovery had led me to a new publisher, one that better fit who I was becoming, and I had released my fourth book, which unabashedly and unapologetically detailed my journey through depression, anxiety, and intensive group therapy. I had let go of relationships and friendships that had been draining my spirit. I had gotten real with myself and with everyone else in my life about who I was, and I had stopped apologizing for who I wasn't. As I shared all these thoughts with my therapist and looked back at how far I had come over the past few years, something beautiful started to happen: I stopped looking at turning forty as a curse and started looking at it as a celebration and even an achievement. I had made it! I had survived!

There is a quote that says, "If life really begins on your fortieth birthday, it's because that's when women finally get it: the guts to take back their lives." I felt like I had taken back my life, from depression and anxiety and settling and disappointing relationships and everything else that had been thrown at me. And I wanted to celebrate it.

About a week before my birthday, I enlisted my friend Laura, and together we did an impromptu photo shoot on my iPhone. I wanted to capture the essence of who I had become in my thirties: a different woman leaving than I was when I started, with a few more battle scars—some visible, some not—but still standing. And better yet: still smiling, perhaps bigger than I had in years, because I had reclaimed myself. I had taken back my life. I had found my joy again. And I couldn't be ending my thirty-ninth year in a better, stronger, more confident place. No, I didn't get to forty un-scathed, but I got there. And that's all that mattered.

Advice I had gotten over the years from friends who hit forty before I did tended to fall into one extreme or the other:

"Forty is when everything falls apart: your body, your eye-sight, your marriage, etc., etc. It's just another stop on the train to old age. Beware! Beware! Beware!"

Or . . .

"Forty is when it all comes together and you tap into your inner strength. You stop worrying about what people think of you, and it's a complete freedom and confidence like you've never known before."

And here is what I now know, having crossed that bridge into my forties myself:

Forty—and any age before or thereafter—will be exactly what you make it. It sounds cliché, but it's true. You can mourn the *what if*s of the end of one decade and chapter, or you can celebrate the beginning of the *what is* of an entirely new decade and chapter. Whichever one you decide to do will set the tone for your forties (or thirties or fifties or six-ties or whatever decade you're in). Forty and frustrated, or forty and fabulous? It's entirely up to you. You have to be willing to release and make peace with all the *what if*s that came before and embrace the *what is* that life has in store.

What do I mean by that? I'll tell you.

When I was in my late twenties and early thirties, I was quite the social butterfly.

I went out almost every Friday and Saturday night, always to the hottest spots in Nashville. I was part of the "it crowd." I even, for a season, belonged to a swanky members-only club. I wore stilettos to work every day and out on the town every night without batting an eye. There were nights when I wouldn't even make it to bed, but then I would still power through an eight-hour workday the next day with nary a yawn. I was never a drinker or crazy partier; I just loved the social scene and going out with my girlfriends, and I was truly living my best life. I couldn't foresee or even imagine a time when that wouldn't be the case.

It's amazing how things change.

Fast-forward to age forty. A few months before the pandemic, there was a period in which I went out two weekends in a row with my girlfriends, which was a rarity for me then and is absolutely unheard of now. The first weekend, we went salsa dancing and I wore my highest, sassiest stilettos for the occasion. In my twenties and thirties, I would have danced a hole in those shoes and then probably worn them to work the next day. But after an hour of stiletto-dancing at age forty, I was ready to take off my heels and toss them in the trash. Which I really might have done except for the fact that my feet were screaming so loudly in pain, I was fearful that when I removed my shoes, I would have nothing but bloody stumps left. By midnight, I was yawning and ready for bed. (Back in my heyday, we didn't even go out until around 11:30 p.m.) After wrangling my girlfriends, I limped pitifully to the car, mentally reassuring myself, *Oh, I didn't get much sleep last night; that's why I can't hang tonight*, because the thought that my life had changed so drastically in a decade that I was defeated by a dance floor and a pair of stilettos was just unacceptable to me. That couldn't be it! There wasn't a dance floor in the city of Nashville I couldn't conquer. (At least, that's what I told myself.)

The next weekend, we went out for a girlfriend's birthday, and this time I wisely wore sandals instead of heels. Downtown Nashville was crawling with people due to a Predators game, and the usual "*whoo*-ing" of bachelorette parties permeated every street corner. It was sheer pandemonium, and we spent more time in the car fighting traffic than we did hanging out. By the time we got to our second destination to see a band, we were so late getting there, we only got to hear two songs. Was I upset about this? No. I was already mentally planning my Netflix lineup once I got home. Once again, I assured myself that it wasn't that I couldn't hang anymore . . . it was just too chaotic downtown for my personal preference. But you know what I realized after reflecting on those two weekends out on the town?

I really just couldn't hang anymore.

And you know what else I realized?

That was okay.

For a long time, perhaps because I'm still single and haven't moved into the "husband and kids" phase of my life, I thought admitting that my tastes had changed and that I didn't enjoy the things I used to enjoy the same way I used to enjoy them made me lame. Or an "oldster." I thought surrendering my penchant for the nightlife and for dancing all night with my girlfriends meant surrendering my youth. I wasn't ready to be like some of the girls I had graduated from high school with, the ones who had all been married and having Tupperware parties for the past twenty years. I wanted to be footloose and fancy free and Forever 21. Admitting that I had grown up and evolved past my twenty- and even thirtysomething self felt a little bit like admitting defeat.

But Forever 21, as we've learned, was just a store, one that didn't fit me anymore, and I wasn't twenty-one or even thirty-one . . . I was forty. And don't get me wrong, I still loved being around my girlfriends. I loved to dance and especially to salsa dance; I just would have been happier to salsa dance for an hour or two and be home in bed by midnight. And I was honored to celebrate my girlfriend's birthday; I just would have been happier to do dinner and skip the traffic and the show and be home in bed by midnight. I hadn't changed that drastically . . . but I had changed . . . and it was time to let myself. It was okay if I didn't have the tolerance to sashay around in high heels for hours on end anymore. I could wear sandals and look just as cute. And it was okay if I needed to call it a night at 10:00. I could have just as much fun in the time that I was there with my girlfriends, even if I excused myself a little early. It was perfectly okay to be this version of Mandy: the version that preferred movie nights at home over checking out the latest hot spot, and coffee shops over nightclubs. *This* Mandy may not make the same choices and like the same things *that* Mandy did, and that is okay.

If you're facing down a milestone birthday, instead of viewing it as losing yourself and all the *what if*s of your youth, how about viewing it as reclaiming yourself and the *what is* of your maturity? Here are a few simple ways to do so:

1. Decide that now is the time to confront your own junk. There's literally no time like the present. Don't take the past with you into one more year. Find a therapist and commit to therapy, because issues are cute when you're a magazine but not so much when

you're a grown woman. You have to stop running
if you have any prayer of finding yourself, your true
self. And you have to be willing to take a good, long
look in the mirror and own every last messy bit of
yourself and your issues if you have any prayer of
becoming the person you're meant to be. So do it. Do
the hard thing. Face the hard truths. And complete
the hard work. It will feel scary and uncomfortable
and sometimes very lonely, but anything—absolutely
anything that's worthwhile in this world—is going
to cost you a little comfort. I'm still very much in the
middle of my process, but I get a little closer to the
woman I want to be every day. Not a perfect woman
. . . but a woman who knows herself. Who accepts
herself. And who is finally at peace with herself. And
that's enough for me.

2. Release toxic/unhealthy relationships. It's time. You
   know the ones I'm talking about. It's hard to embrace who you are becoming if you're surrounded
   by people who want you to stay as you are. Relationships that do not support and encourage your growth
   are not healthy. Let them go.

3. Get real with yourself and with the people in your
   life. Stop apologizing for who you are, your hopes,
   your dreams, your politics, your religion, your goals,
   etc. Ask yourself, *Am I in the career that most brings
   me to life?* And if the answer is no, start looking for
   the thing you really want to do. The thing that lights
   you up inside. Life is too short to spend it chained to
   someone else's desk or living someone else's dream.

Plan that trip you've always wanted to take. Start exploring adoption if you're like me and still single but want to be a mom. A milestone birthday is the perfect time to take inventory of your life and start doing and being the things you always dreamed of.

4. Finally . . . look back with gratitude, not regret. Where you've been doesn't define you. The only thing that matters is here and now, and you are right where you are meant to be. Trust your path and where it has brought you. That way, when it's time to say goodbye to one age and hello to another, you'll be ready to smile and say, "Thank u, next."

If you're in a new season or a new chapter of life and you're having a hard time adjusting to or accepting this new, different version of you, I want to encourage you to go a little easier on yourself. So maybe you're not the twentysomething or thirtysomething or even fortysomething you once were . . . but guess what? You're the person that twentysomething and thirtysomething and fortysomething fought hard to become. And it is enough. We are allowed to outgrow people in this life, and that includes outgrowing past versions of ourselves. You wouldn't try to force a stiletto that didn't fit (or a sandal . . . *ha!*), so why try to force a life that no longer fits? Own where you are and who you are in this moment because she may not be Forever 21, but she's pretty darn awesome. And without those previous versions of you, you would have never gotten to the here-and-now version of you. Every past version of you was exactly who and what you needed to be at that moment, and you did the best you could at the time and it was enough. But those moments have passed. It's okay to let them go and turn toward a new day. It's okay to release the *what if*s of who you once hoped to be and just relish the *what is* that you are.

Because, at the end of the day, you can walk tall in any shoes as long as you love and embrace every version of you.

12

Navigating Adult Friendships

I n the last chapter, we talked about the importance of letting go of past versions of yourself and how, in order to do that, sometimes you have to let go of other people who are no longer good for you. In these next couple of chapters, I want to dive a little deeper into exactly who those people are—starting with friendships.

There is a quote floating around online that says, "I no longer have the energy for meaningless friendships, forced interactions, or unnecessary conversations." Don't ask me who the author is because I couldn't tell you. But at this stage in my life, I feel this quote deep in my soul.

A few years ago, when I was struggling to get over a breakup and avoiding being alone at all costs, I would make plans with a potted plant if it would keep me busy and occupied and not lost in my own thoughts. I did not discriminate.

Known you for a week? Let's hang out. Met you on Bumble BFF five minutes ago? Let's go to dinner. Random person who hit me up on Facebook because you're a fan of my books and for all I know you could be a serial killer? Sure, I'll have coffee with you! I kid, but I didn't have much of a vetting process when it came to whom I allowed into my life. And to be honest, I don't think I valued myself or my time very much during that season. I was on the go constantly. But much like a hamster in a wheel, I was always running but not really getting anywhere.

But then the pandemic happened, and I spent the greater part of a year alone. I learned that I wouldn't die from loneliness, and I learned that I actually enjoyed my own company.

And then everything with my parents happened, and I was surprised and dismayed to see the response from people I knew. It takes only a few seconds to send a text checking in on someone, and during those long early months of struggle and sadness and anxiety right after Mom's and Dad's diagnoses, I had only one friend who did that, almost every single day. It was my friend of more than twenty years, Laura, who has stood by me through thick and thin, and I am eternally grateful for her and her unwavering support and friendship. Some friends checked in every few weeks, and that meant something to me, even if I didn't hear from them as often. But others? As for some, I knew it was time to move on. I'm proud of myself for setting that boundary and sticking to it. I could have *what if*-ed myself until the end of time—*What if they just don't understand how bad things are?* or *What if they don't know what to say?* or *What if I'm being too harsh?*—but I had to let go of the *what ifs* and look at the *what is.* And the silence told me everything I needed to know about the friendship.

Years of therapy and introspection and doing the hard work on myself have completely changed my perspective on friendship. (I'm sure getting older has helped enlighten me some too.) Today, I don't have the desire or the energy to keep investing in people who aren't investing in me.

The majority of the people I consider my closest confidants have been in my life for at least seven or eight years or more. My lifelong friend Jason says you have to walk through all four seasons with someone, a friend or a romantic prospect, to know if they are someone worthy of being in your life forever. I don't know if that's true or if there's an exact formula to it, but I do know that as I get older, it becomes more and more vital for me to have people in my life with whom I have roots. People who have known me since before I was even *me.* People I know I can trust with absolutely anything: the good, the bad, and the ugly. People I can be vulnerable with and be messy with and be 100 percent myself with, who I know will always have my back no matter what I say or do or what mistakes I make. People who will never fail to show up for me when the bottom drops out of my life and my most feared *what if* becomes my *what is.* People who never let me linger too long in the shadows but who always take my hand and turn me back toward the sun.

I don't want to force friendship anymore either. I don't want to have to stay on your radar or in your line of sight or constantly be the one calling and inviting and initiating the friendship. If you can't meet me halfway, maybe you shouldn't meet me at all. I know life can get hectic and we all get busy . . . but nobody is *that* busy. If our friendship exists only because I am the one doing all the work and all the heavy lifting, then I'm okay with opening my hand and letting you slide right on through my fingers. That isn't meant to sound harsh. I will love you and wish good things for you, but I won't chase you. I value my time too much. I value myself too much. And I know what I bring to the table as a friend, so I'm not afraid to eat alone.

I say all this to say . . . adult friendships are hard. Making time for our friends can be challenging, especially when you're juggling work and/or kids, marriage, and all the other responsibilities that come along with adulting. But friendship is just like anything else in life. The greater the investment, the greater the reward. And "too busy" is a myth. People make time for the things (and people) that are important to them.

Which brings me to this point: Hold yourself just as accountable as you do your friends. You have to be willing to check yourself too. Are you being a good friend? Are you making the effort? Are you calling and texting and checking in? Are you showing up for your friends when they're going through especially challenging seasons?

In short—are you being a flake, or are you being a friend?

Let's face it, y'all: We're living in an age of *un*accountability, and people are flakier than the breakfast cereal I pour into my bowl every morning. (And, yes, if you feel like I'm talking to you, I probably am.)

Unaccountability means what, exactly? Well, to make myself sound really ancient, back in the day when you had to cancel plans, you didn't get to just shoot someone a text and bail (because texting didn't exist), and the idea of just ghosting someone and not showing up was unheard of (because:

manners). When you made plans with someone—friend or romantic pursuit—you could revel in those plans, look forward to those plans, get excited about those plans. Because those plans—barring a major emergency—were pretty much set in stone.

In the new roaring twenties, however, both a vague one-sentence text bailing on plans *and* simply ghosting and not showing up are both options some people deem viable. Making plans with someone and those plans actually being followed through on are about as much of a "certainty" as winning the lottery. I mean . . . I haven't done the math, but I'd almost be willing to bet you'd be *more* likely to win the lottery than to have every plan you make within a given week actually come to fruition. There's no face-to-face or even voice-to-voice interaction, no awkwardness, no muss, no fuss, and zero accountability. You can just send the text and go about your day without ever having to contend with how your flakiness might be impacting the other person.

Is canceling plans really that big of a deal in the grand scheme of things? *Yes.* Let me qualify that. If a last-minute emergency or unavoidable family conflict or something genuinely pressing comes up every once in a while that forces you to cancel plans, that is completely and totally understandable. We all have things come up, and you have to have some grace and flexibility in your friendships. But if you are canceling plans because a boy was mean to you or because you decided at the last minute you needed to wash your hair or for any other wishy-washy (pun intended), lame reason . . . that is not okay. That's not to say you shouldn't take self-care days, because you absolutely should. But you should also have enough care and concern and respect for your friendships that you don't decide thirty minutes before you're set to meet someone that your self-care day should take precedence over your commitment to your friend. And here's the thing you need to remember, too, if you are married or in a relationship or have kids or all of the above and you're canceling plans with a single friend: You tend to have built-in and consistent community in that you at least have kids or a significant other. There's a good chance that *you* were the community for the week for the person you just canceled on, and they likely had been looking forward to spending time with you all week. And now you've bailed on them at the last minute, giving them no time to make other plans and essentially stripping them of their community for the week. So, *yes*, it is a really big deal to cancel plans, and it might impact the other person's mental health in ways you can't possibly see in the moment you shoot off a one-line text message standing them up.

I can honestly say, when I make plans nowadays, I usually give it a 50 percent chance that those plans will take place. I know I'm not alone in this, and the problem isn't that I have really crappy friends. The problem is that people, in general, don't put in enough effort when it comes to friendship in this day and age. We don't take commitment seriously, and by "commitment," I mean commitment to our word and to doing what we say we're going to do. We view relationships as disposable and easy come, easy go. And we're more concerned with our comfort and convenience than we are our character and integrity. We prefer to stay safely behind the *what if* of our phone screens than to show up for the *what is* and do the work of being a good friend. And that has to stop. I know the pandemic made things a little weird, guys, but c'mon. People were bailing on plans right and left long before Covid came to town.

So what can you do to stop being a flake and start being a friend? It's simple actually.

1. Don't be halfhearted. If you make plans with someone, make every possible effort to see those plans through. Barring an emergency, *show up*. Chances are, even if you feel like canceling because of a long week or whatever, you'll have a great time once you get there and be glad you didn't bail.

2. If you see a few days in advance that you're going to have to cancel, go ahead and cancel instead of waiting until the last minute. Respect the other person's time. Give the other person some lead time, especially if it's on a weekend, so they can make other plans. Again, for us singles, sometimes the only community we have all week is with you . . . and if you flake on us at the last minute, we have to go another week without that community.

3. If you do cancel plans, make every effort to reschedule. About a month or so ago, I had someone text me (at the last minute) to cancel plans that had been on my calendar for over a month. I texted back to say I'd love to reschedule . . . and I haven't heard back since. Having to cancel plans is one thing, but failing to respond to someone when they let you know they want to reschedule is just not okay. No one is that busy, y'all.

4. Never ghost someone. *Never*. This is never, ever okay. If you have to cancel on someone at the last minute,

you should have the decency to pick up the phone and call them, not send a halfhearted text or just ghost altogether. Always treat people with the same respect you would want someone to treat you with.

5. Realize that to have a friend, you have to be a friend. If you are consistently flaky and unreliable, eventually people are going to stop making plans with you. And the only person you will have to blame is you. I have people in my own life whom I love but keep at arm's length because I'm tired of allowing them to disappoint me. You will always get back what you put out when it comes to friendship.

At the end of the day, flakes are cute in a cereal box but not so much in life. If you're constantly canceling plans, step up your friendship game! Hold yourself to the same standard you set for your friends. And if you have someone who consistently lets you down and cancels on you and doesn't show up for you, it might be time to surrender all the *what if*s you have in your head about who you *think* this person is and take a good long look at who they really are. Are they talking the talk, or walking the walk? Friendship is a wonderful, beautiful thing . . . but much like a romantic relationship, it shouldn't be that hard. If they can't see what a blessing it is to have you as a friend, maybe they shouldn't have you at all.

Ultimately, you get to set the friendship standard in your life. You get to decide when to stay and when to call it a day and walk away. My new friendship manifesto is simple: I don't force or chase. If our friendship ends because I stop calling or texting you, we weren't good friends to begin with and I'm okay with letting you go. And boundaries are firmly in place until I know for sure you're a safe person, someone with whom I can share my innermost thoughts and biggest heartbreaks, my biggest wins and my biggest losses, and you won't flinch or judge or bail. I would encourage you to establish your own friendship manifesto and not be afraid to stick to it. You might find that certain people drop out of your life when you do. But the really cool thing is, those departures make room for the new people who are going to appear. I'm a firm believer in the idea that everyone who is meant to be in our lives will be in our lives, and the ones who aren't will go.

And either way . . . we'll be okay.

13

Decoding Mysterious Male Behavior

Why Sometimes Going Is Better Than Knowing

We cracked the code earlier on when to let go in love, and we've just covered when to let go in friendship . . . but what about when to let go in the early stages of dating? Especially for those of us who might have stepped away from dating for long periods of time—say, in the midst of a global pandemic. Taking the plunge back into the dating pool after an extended hiatus can feel a lot like trying to learn how to ride a unicycle: wobbly, unsure, and absolutely terrifying. Not to mention it's fraught with *what ifs*. *What if I don't match with anyone? What if I've forgotten how to act on a date? What if things have changed so drastically in my time away from dating that I have no idea how to relate to men? WHAT IF, WHAT IF, WHAT IF?!* Well, as someone who has started to ever-so-slightly dip her toe back into the dating baby pool after almost two years away, I'm happy to report that *what is* is that men are just as weird and mysterious as ever. Much the way the groundhog, after a long winter's nap, emerges from his hovel, takes a quick look around, and frustratingly declares that winter is not quite over . . . it's like men emerged from their pandemic hole, stretched, looked around, and frustratingly declared that baffling male behaviors are not quite over. While it might seem at times like I am giving our gentlemen friends a hard time, that is 100 percent not my intent. I truly do adore the menfolk in all their mysterious maleness. Please understand that when I point out the quirky weirdness and random behaviors of our dude counterparts, it is always done in fun and for the sake of humor. Unless, of course, I'm telling the story of how a guy was a jerk or a ghoster or a flake, and then, yes, I am totally and unabashedly calling him out for it. But even in that case, I'm just being sassy—not male-bashy!

Now that we've gotten that out of the way, let's dive into a subject that is frequently the main topic of discussion among me and my single girlfriends: mysterious male behavior. Like the guy who double-booked me for an entire weekend and then stood me up both nights. Or the one I've referenced in previous books with whom I had the most perfect first date ever—only to have him turn around and ask me for twenty dollars at the end of the date. (When I agreed to go out with him, I wasn't under the impression that I would be charged at the end of the date.) Or the guy who . . . are you ready for this? . . . GOT VACCINATED FOR ME AND

THEN GHOSTED ME THREE DAYS LATER. Yep, the post-pandemic mysterious male behavior is perhaps even more baffling than pre-pandemic. Allow me to tell you the story.

Remember the good old days, way back in 2019, when dating was as simple as swiping right or sliding into the DMs to make a love connection? The days when "meeting for coffee" actually meant meeting in a coffee shop and not in some random outdoor space complete with mask, hand sanitizer, a second mask for good measure, and matching vaccination cards? Yep, 2020 added a whole new layer of awkwardness and weirdness to the already-awkward weirdness that is modern dating.

Modern dating—and by "modern," I mean since the invention of dating apps—is a necessary evil that all of us who find ourselves still consciously uncoupled way past the point we ever planned to be must endure. Much like anything else in life, it has its glorious highs, its awesomely bad lows, and its moments of downright hilarity. After a while, you learn to go with the flow and ride the *what ifs* and waves of uncertainty, buoyed along by the various *what is* success stories you hear from friends about their friend whose friend's friend swiped right on their soulmate and now they're living happily ever after. But throw in a global pandemic, and you go from riding the waves to, like . . . *Sharknado*. All of a sudden we had to worry less about whether we'd catch feelings for someone and more about whether we'd catch coronavirus from them.

If you're anything like me—and by that, I mean you spent the majority of the pandemic hiding out in a cloud of Lysol like Sheldon Cooper in that famous gif—your efforts to avoid getting sick might have caused your dating life to take a bit of a hit. I mean, it got to the point where a lot of us had been in more lockdowns than relationships. And while the extroverted side of me missed the talking and the texting and the bantering and the flirting that come along with dating, my inner introvert, who prefers Netflix and nap to Netflix and chill, secretly reveled in the endless amounts of solitude to read and watch movies while wearing pj's 24/7 and eating ice cream straight from the carton. In a contest to see which caused me more anxiety, the pandemic or modern dating, I'm not sure which one would come out on top.

So in March 2021, when a guy I knew vaguely from my hometown reached out to me and asked if I wanted to meet for coffee, I felt a myriad of emotions. Uncertainty. Anxiety. Hesitation. But also . . . could it be? A hint of excitement. For the past year, the only male energy I had had in my life belonged to my dad and my cat. The idea of resurrecting my dating life, albeit from six feet apart, intrigued me enough to agree to a meet-up. (Outside and from the responsible aforementioned six feet apart. Things with Covid were still pretty hairy, and I wasn't taking any chances.)

Headed to that first meeting, I was super nervous. I hadn't been out on a date in well over a year and a half. For that matter, I had barely had any human contact at all outside of my parents for a year. What if I couldn't remember how to make small talk? How to banter? How to flirt? Since most of my social interactions took place on social media throughout the pandemic, I wondered if I could just sit there silently and hold up flash cards with emojis on them to communicate so I would feel like I was in my safe space. Or had I truly become the unsocialized cavewoman who would just grunt and gesture and hope he understood?

Despite all my many *what if*s, as it turned out, dating really was like riding a bike. Within the first few minutes, we fell into a comfortable back and forth, and my nerves eased. We laughed a lot, the conversation flowed easily, and an hour passed quickly. And when he said, "We should do this again sometime," I agreed. I made it clear what my boundaries were and that I wouldn't be comfortable hanging out indoors until I was fully vaccinated but that I would be totally down to meet up outdoors again soon. And I *thought* he got the message.

Until I realized he very much did not.

After that first meet-up, he started calling and texting. A lot. It was a bit of a shock to the system to go from not dating or even talking to a guy for a year and a half to hearing from one every five minutes, all day long. I tried to roll with it, but internally my gut was ringing the alarm. It felt like way too much, too soon. He also kept suggesting he cook me dinner, which in ordinary times would be great. But in the time of Covid, when I had two high-risk parents to protect, it felt like a bad idea. I had come this far and I was days away from my first vaccination. To take unnecessary chances would be like running the entire Boston Marathon only to stop inches from the finish line. After the fourth or fifth time he brought it up, I realized I needed to be more clear and firm about my boundaries. I explained in no uncertain terms, again, why I wouldn't be comfortable hanging out indoors until I was fully vaccinated. "Even better if you're fully vaccinated too . . . but that's your call to make," I said.

Within five minutes of that conversation—and this is not an exaggeration—he had made his first vaccination appointment. "Now do you see how serious I am about getting to go out with you?" he texted. "You're so worth waiting for."

Wow, I thought. Now *this* is romance! Forget Noah and Allie and "If you're a bird, I'm a bird." Forget Jack and Rose and "If you jump, I jump." I had "If you're vaccinated against a deadly global airborne disease, I'm vaccinated against a deadly global airborne disease" guy! Love in the time of Covid, indeed!

"I bet I'm the first guy to ever get a deadly-virus vaccine to get to go out with you!" he crowed via text message, including a snapshot of his vaccination card.

He definitely was.

He also has the distinct honor of being the first guy to ever get a deadly-virus vaccine to get to go out with me . . . only to ghost me three days later.

Yep. If this brief romance was like *Titanic*, this time *he* was Rose and *I* was Jack, and he shoved me right off the bed frame into the freezing cold waters of rejection—*after getting vaccinated for me*. This definitely took mysterious male behavior to the next level.

I've been ghosted plenty of times in my life but never by someone who went to such extremes to go out with me in the first place. In hindsight, there were loads of red flags: He was way too pushy and eager way too quickly (one night I didn't respond to one text so he texted three more times, called me, then called me again first thing the next morning); he called me "babe" and "sweetheart" in the first two weeks; and, I mean, last but certainly not least, he got vaccinated for me before we ever had so much as a second date.

The irony of the fact that I had just written a book about dating, only to get ghosted by a guy who got vaccinated for me, was not lost on me. It was almost downright poetic. I wrote a book about dating and yet I had a carton of milk in my fridge that lasted longer than my first "relationship" back out there again post-lockdown. But as I said in *Don't Believe the Swipe*, ghosting says nothing about me and everything about the other person.[1] He obviously wasn't mature enough to handle an adult relationship, and that was on him . . . not me.

And *hey*! At least I helped get one more person vaccinated. Right?!

I could go on and on with the list of mysterious male behaviors that my girlfriends and I have been witnesses to over the years, Vaccination Ghost not even being the most bizarre. And if we added all of *your* experiences to the list, we could fill the rest of this book (and likely my next four or five books as well). But what it boils down to is this: Sometimes guys are just *weird*, y'all. And no amount of investigating or rereading *Men Are from Mars, Women Are from Venus* or banging our heads against the wall trying to understand their baffling ways will bring us any closer to understanding them.

For example, why do some dudes think posing with a dead (and often bloody) deer or turkey carcass on their dating profile is cute? I mean . . . I get that hunting is a thing. It's not *my* thing, but I totally get that it's a thing that people do. And that's fine (as long as you are hunting for food and not for sport). My point is not to make some antihunting statement here, so don't come for me, hunters. My point is to ask, Why on God's green earth do men think that any woman would say, "Yep, sign me uppppp!" to a photo of a man spooning a bloody animal carcass?! Do they not know us at all? (Don't answer that.) We would be much more impressed by a cute photo of him snuggling with his (live) dog. Dogfish me allllll day long, fellas. But deadturkeyfishing? No, thank you.

And why do men with less-than-honorable intentions on dating apps always start off their cringey commentary with "Are you affectionate?" Yes, this is an actual thing, ladies. If a man asks you this, just go ahead and unmatch because his questions are about to take a very NC-17 turn. I found this out the hard way when I got on my first dating app. And then again a few more times, because it took me a minute to connect the "Are you affectionate?" question with the Creepers Are Us questions that would follow. I'm not sure if there's like a secret society of men who get together and discuss ways to subtly shift online conversations from flirty to dirty, but the fact that they all use this same lead-in is weird and bewildering and completely inexplicable.

And while we're on the subject of secret societies of men . . . is there also one that teaches guys how to instinctively know when their ex has moved on, and that it's time to pop back up again in her life, completely arbitrarily, in an attempt to stop her from moving on? *Like how do they always know?* It feels like the worst boomerang ever when a guy you've spent months putting out of your heart and mind picks that precise moment to slide back into your DMs and your life. It happens every single time! They always come back, and always at the most inopportune times. This superhuman sixth sense that men seem to have for picking the exact moment you've finally left them in your rearview mirror to cruise back into your life is one of the most mysterious of the mysterious male behaviors. And to be honest, we will likely never know how they know.

And why do men in their thirties and forties and beyond seem determined to just "hang out" for all eternity? What happened to actual . . . dating? Guys, listen. I don't need you to roll out a red carpet for me or take me to the most expensive restaurant in town. I don't need or even want "fancy" at this point in my life. I don't need you to jump through hoops or buy me expensive gifts or be extra in any way at all. To be honest, extra and over-the-top gestures don't ring true to me and I want no part of them. I'm a pretty simple girl and a grown woman all in one, and it's the little things that impress me. The biggest little thing that impresses me is effort. I don't think it's too much to ask for a little effort. You don't have to strain yourself or break the bank or go out of your way to put in a little effort and actually plan a *date* (a date, in case you don't know, is a social or romantic appointment or engagement) instead of sending a halfhearted text asking me to "hang out." I'm forty-two. I don't want to hang out! I'm tired of hanging out. I don't care if the date is going for ice cream or coffee or on a walk or to the movies or wherever it may be—put in a little effort. Effort is attractive. Effort shows me you value your time with me. And effort is so simple. We're not asking you to lasso the moon here, fellas. As ladies, we just want to see that we are worth your time and effort. The littlest things and the smallest gestures truly do go so far.

We will likely never have answers to *any* of these mysterious male behaviors, like why a man gets vaccinated for a woman he turns right around and ghosts three days later. Or why he chooses to ghost at all. Or why he chooses to come back, for that matter. And I don't think we'll ever have an explanation for why he would choose to ask you for twenty dollars at the end of a date. And if you're a type-A control freak like me, the lack of clarity and endless *what if*s in dating can be frustrating and disconcerting. Like, we're supposed to just . . . accept . . . these random occurrences as random occurrences instead of trying to find the order in all the randomness? Women tend to be as stubbornly persistent as the *Scooby-Doo* gang when it comes to wanting answers and wanting clarity and wanting understanding and wanting to solve the mystery. We will dig and search and inspect and investigate and rack our brains for clues to answer the unanswerable. Women love clarity as much as we love closure. But, unlike those meddling *Scooby-Doo* kids, most of the time we won't have the opportunity to whisk off a guy's ghost mask and find the answers as to why he ghosted us. Some mysteries of the universe and of the male mind are simply unsolvable, and either you can drive yourself crazy trying to be in the know, or you can simply let go and move on with the show. (I hear from my male friends all the time that we womenfolk are just as inexplicable and mysterious . . . and I don't doubt for a second that it's true! But alas, I can only speak from the female perspective on this one.)

Now don't misunderstand me here. Certainly if someone you've been with for a significant amount of time disappears or betrays you or randomly asks you for twenty dollars at the end of your one-year-anniversary dinner, you've earned the right to ask for clarity. But most mysterious male behaviors in the beginning of a relationship simply aren't worth trying to get to the bottom of. Your peace is more important than driving yourself crazy trying to understand why something happened the way it did. Let it go. If you're spending more time trying to figure someone out than you are getting to know them, it's time to call off the investigation and move on with your life. Dating and relationships shouldn't be that hard. If it doesn't flow, let go of your need to know, and *go*. It is as simple as that.

The early stage of getting to know someone should be fun; it shouldn't be torture. Or confusing. Or frustrating. And it shouldn't feel like a live-action game of Clue either: "It was Colonel Mustard on Bumble with the dagger . . . to my heart." If he comes with more mystery than magic, you might have to accept that it's not meant to be and move on. Pull yourself out of the *what ifs* and look at *what is*: What is he doing and saying rather than what is it you want him to be doing or saying or hope he'll do or say? In the *what is* lies most of the answers to even the most mysterious of male behaviors.

And remember this: There *are* guys out there who will be clear and intentional and straightforward with their feelings for you, no Scooby Snacks required. For a long time in my life, I thought mystery in a man was attractive. I even dubbed my longtime on-again, off-again ex "Mr. E" because of the fact that he was such a "mystery." But as I've gotten older, I've realized that there's nothing cute about keeping someone guessing and leaving them stuck in the endless gray area of *what if*, whether it be about your feelings or your intentions or your character or whatever. Clear-cut and open and honest appeal to me these days. So let's make men of mystery history . . . yes? And free up space in our lives and our hearts for love that comes with more answers than questions. Because it is out there. And you won't have to be a private investigator to find it.

14

Anxiety

The What If behind the Curtain

Life comes with a whole lot of *what if*s. From our health to our faith to our friendships to our love lives, there are far more questions than answers in just about every major aspect of life. And it's human nature to want to answer all the questions, dot all the i's and cross all the t's, neutralize the unknowns, and control the uncontrollable. When we inevitably can't do any of those things, it leads to anxiety.

I came across a meme the other day that said something to the effect of "Welcome to middle age. If you don't already have an anxiety disorder, one will be assigned to you," and I've never read anything more true. If the past couple of years have taught us anything, it's that we live in an anxiety-driven world: the urgency of social media feeding us a constant stream of negative news stories as they happen; technology designed to connect us that leaves us increasingly disconnected; traffic, bills, telemarketers, deadlines, and unread emails; even something as simple as buying a movie ticket to veg out in front of the big screen turns into a fight to the finish since you only have a certain number of seconds to complete your order before someone else takes your seat.

Then, thrown in on top of all the day-to-day stressors we're already contending with: a deadly global pandemic that uprooted pretty much everyone from their "normal" and forced us all to find new ways to live and work and socialize and cope for more than a year. The mental and emotional toll is still playing out today and probably will be for quite some time.

Anxiety is at an all-time high, and it's easy to find yourself stressed out, overwhelmed, tensed up, and overcaffeinated just to keep up with it all. And then all the caffeine only leads to the jitters, which leads to more anxiety, until you're on the Stress Express and there's no turning back.

Though I gave up caffeine several years ago in the name of calmness, anxiety has been a part of my reality for as long as I can remember. I had my first identifiable panic attack when I was in college, but when I look back now at my teen and childhood years, I can pinpoint several other episodes that would certainly qualify as panic attacks; I just didn't know what to call them at the time. I've been extremely open and transparent about my struggles, even dedicating one entire book to my journey through anxiety and depression.[1] But what I perhaps haven't been quite as open about is the shame I carried for a really, really long time about those struggles. The way my anxiety so often made me feel weak and flawed and damaged and even . . . unlovable. You see, much like its twisted sister depression, anxiety is a liar. It's the ultimate *what if*. It wants to make you believe that everything is scary, nothing and no one can be trusted (especially not yourself), and you're in danger at all times. It's the bully on the playground that will use your own thoughts against you: *What if this happens? What if that happens? What if I have a panic attack in front of everyone and embarrass myself? What if I'm going crazy? What if I'm having a heart attack? What if my anxiety stops me from ever being able to find love? What if I'm irreparably broken? WHAT IF, WHAT IF, WHAT IF?!* It has you so focused on all the imagined *what if*s that you are blinded to the *what is* right in front of you: You are fine; the worst-case scenario almost never happens; your body is in fight-or-flight mode; your anxiety doesn't define you—it's just an annoying part of yourself that you have to learn to coexist with; and, most importantly, you *can* handle whatever happens and whatever life throws at you. Because anxiety, more than anything, wants you to believe that you can't. That you'll just fall apart and go curl up in the fetal position in the corner and that will be the end of your story.

Guess what? Even as someone with intense anxiety and two different diagnosed anxiety disorders, I have never once fallen apart so badly I couldn't be put back together. I have never once failed to meet the moment. I have never once curled up in the fetal position in the corner. Maybe you have, and that's okay. Because all that really matters is that you got back up again. (And you *did* get back up again, or you wouldn't be reading this book.)

Anxiety wants to keep you in the shadows of fear and worry and panic and self-doubt, because it can only exist in the dark. Anxiety wants you to believe it's the great big, terrifying, all-powerful Wizard of Oz . . . but it's really just the small, scared, ineffectual man behind the curtain. Anxiety wants to do everything in its power to keep you from turning toward the sun because, much like a cockroach, it knows that when it is exposed to the light of you stepping into your own power, it will be forced to flee. The way anxiety maintains its stronghold on your life is through shame. If you're too embarrassed and ashamed to admit you're struggling and seek help, anxiety wins. And if you're too embarrassed and ashamed to later share your story so that you can turn right around and pull someone else who's struggling into the sun with you, anxiety keeps winning.

I'm here to tell you that anxiety isn't winning anything today—*not on my watch*.

After the triple whammy of the pandemic, then Dad's diagnosis, then Mom's diagnosis, my anxiety began to slowly spiral out of control. I held it together and powered through for a solid two months after that awful night in September 2020 when we first got the call about Mom, but after she was put in the hospital in November with pneumonia, I could feel the familiar vise of panic and fear start to tighten around me. This time, it manifested in a new way: health anxiety. (If you suffer from anxiety, I'm sure you're familiar with how it just loves to morph and evolve into new levels and new devils.) I had always been a little nervous about health-related stuff—I mean, is anyone super Zen about going to the doctor? And during the pandemic, my health anxiety had skyrocketed even more. But after Mom and Dad were both diagnosed with cancer, it began to spiral completely out of control. I was terrified that, like the old superstition goes, bad things were going to come in threes, and I would be the next person in our family to be diagnosed with a terrible disease. Living with the constant fear of the pandemic, coupled with the now-ever-present worry and fear about Mom and Dad, had begun to feel like we were unwilling stars of the latest installment of the horror film *Final Destination*—constantly trying to outrun and cheat death. It left me exhausted, overwhelmed, and hyperaware of and focused on my body. Suddenly every little ache and pain was cause for alarm. The *what if*s began to consume me. *What if I have cancer too? What if I have to undergo treatment by myself because Mom and Dad can't be there for me? What if I can't be there to help Mom and Dad? What if I'm sick or dying? WHAT IF, WHAT IF, WHAT IF?!* I was completely trapped in my thoughts with no ability to reason with myself or see the reality of my *what is*: I was forty-two years old with all the normal body sensations that come along with being forty-two years old, and I had just watched my parents get diagnosed with cancer, one right after the other. Of course I was going to feel vulnerable and afraid.

By December 2020, my anxiety had heightened to the point where I had very little quality of life or ability to be helpful to Mom and Dad because my anxious thoughts and all the *what if*s playing in my head all day like a broken record were eating me alive. And it wasn't like I could get out of the house and go to the movies or go get my nails done or hang out with my girlfriends to get out of my head, because the pandemic was raging and everyone was on high alert. I was stuck inside a perfect storm of anxiety, and I knew the only way out was to seek help.

Although I had maintained my weekly therapy sessions the entire time, I had reached the point where I knew I needed something more intensive. So I had a very honest conversation with my therapist, and she agreed, even offering me a few referrals. After doing some research, I settled on a treatment program that kicked off in January 2021. I would attend therapy online every day, five days a week, for five hours a day. It was a big commitment, especially in light of the fact that I was helping to care for Mom and Dad. But I knew if I didn't take the measures I needed to take to get my anxiety under control, I wouldn't be of any use to them or myself. I had to find a way to release the *what ifs* that were controlling me and step back into the *what is*.

So that's what I did.

Every day for two solid months, I showed up (to my computer screen) and did the hard work. Again. For the third time in my life, I was in intensive daily therapy. I knew it would work because it had always worked in the past. And even though I was relieved and excited and ready to really dig in and do the work and get my life back on track, I couldn't help but feel ashamed and like a bit of a failure that I had found myself right back in the same place . . . again.

What if I have to undergo intensive treatment every few years for the rest of my life? What if my anxiety never really goes away? What if I have to resign myself to this being my story?

I was having anxiety . . . about my anxiety. I felt small and broken and embarrassed and weak.

But as the days in treatment went on and I spent hours each day (albeit through a computer screen) with other people who were struggling with the same issues I was, little by little, I began to reframe all my many *what if*s. I didn't look at any of the people in my group as small or broken or weak. I didn't see any reason for *them* to be embarrassed or ashamed. I actually looked at them as really incredibly strong for having the courage not just to ask for help but to actively seek it, even when it was painful, even when it was hard, even when it was uncomfortable. So why was I not showing myself the same grace or viewing myself through the same lens?

And so what if I *did* have to undergo intensive treatment every few years? What if my anxiety really never *did* go away? Anxiety might very well be a medical condition, just like asthma or diabetes or lupus, that I might live with and learn to manage for the rest of my life. So what if this was the case and anxiety *was* just destined to be a part of my story forever? Was that really the end of the world?

The truth is, short of a miraculous intervention from God, my anxiety most likely will be with me for the rest of my life. It's not who I am, but it is a *part* of who I am. It's not a part that I love, but neither is it a badge of shame. Anxious people are deeply sensitive, empathetic, passionate people who feel things so strongly that sometimes our bodies just become overwhelmed with all the emotions. We are intense and powerful and imaginative creatures whose superpower happens to be our ability to *feel*. And is that really a bad thing? Sure, our hearts might sometimes race and our palms might sweat and our minds might overthink and our nervous systems might overwork, but aren't all these also glorious signs that we are deeply, deeply *alive*? I don't know about you, but I'd rather feel too much than too little—all day, every day. And if the price I have to pay to be an intensely alive, feeling person is an intensive therapeutic tune-up every few years, I'll take it. Maybe my story was never meant to be one of a girl who boldly took on all of life's challenges and *what if*s without fear or flinching, but that of a girl who was absolutely terrified of the challenges and *what if*s and still showed up every single day to her life anyway and did it afraid. She persevered. Isn't that the mark of true courage? It's not brave to turn toward the sun when the sun is all you've ever known. But it's downright audacious to turn toward the sun when the storm of fear and anxiety and panic is raging all around you.

There is one thing I want to insert here that I think is so very, very important for people of faith to hear: It's okay to have Jesus and anxiety too. It's okay to have Jesus and depression too. It's okay to have Jesus and a therapist too. And it's okay to have Jesus and medication too.

At times in the past, people I've opened up to, either online or in person, about the fact that I was struggling with anxiety have responded with a glib "God's got this! Don't give in to anxiety! Do what you were born to do!" Being real and transparent about my struggles *is* the thing that God called me to do. You can fully believe that God does indeed have this and still be scared. And still recognize that God has had all situations since the beginning of time, and still bad things have happened. People are lost. Cancer and wars and famine and unrest and earthquakes and tornadoes and pandemics are all still a thing, even though "God's got this."

So the point I'm making is this: God can be holding you in the palm of His hand, and simultaneously you can still have anxiety. Both things can be true at the same time. You are who you are, and it is okay. You feel what you feel, and it is okay. And you do whatever it is you need to do to heal, and it is okay. God gave us doctors for a reason. It doesn't make you weak or lacking in faith because you're choosing faith *and* works. Absolutely, pray about your anxiety or your depression or any other mental health issue you struggle with, but don't hesitate to take steps and seek professional help to learn to manage those struggles. And anyone who doesn't like it or who thinks that your taking an active role in your own health and well-being is a "lack of faith" can kindly see themselves off your friends list and out of your life. Don't let anyone shame you or bully you into feeling like anything you're doing to get through the day is wrong.

Because here's the thing: That whole "waiting in faith" and "trusting God" and "peace that surpasses understanding" thing? It tends to all fly right out the window when I'm anxious. I turn into a complete and total doubting Thomas. I used to be embarrassed and ashamed of how "weak" I would become in those big, scary moments. But then I remembered the love and care and gentleness that Jesus showed Thomas during his moments of fear and doubt, and I realized He views me the same way. Why did God even choose to share Thomas's story with us? I think it's because He wanted us to know that it's okay for us to be afraid. It's okay for us to even doubt Him at times. It's okay for us to be anxious and unsure. He can handle it. He is big enough to love us right through it. And if the God of the universe can see us and know us and love us right where we are, shouldn't we be able to love ourselves and show ourselves the same immense love and grace and acceptance He shows us?

I'm happy to report that my third time in intensive therapy not only helped me untangle all the knots of fear that had accumulated in my life throughout the pandemic and Mom's and Dad's battles with cancer; it also helped me learn to accept my anxiety and coexist with it a little more graciously, once and for all. I will never view anxiety as a best friend that I will roll out the welcome wagon for, but I can accept it as an occasional roommate I might have to begrudgingly put up with when times get tough. Because as you may recall from *The Wizard of Oz*, the man behind the curtain was misguided and manipulative and even downright dishonest, but he wasn't all bad. Once Dorothy and friends were able to really see him in the light of day and accept him for the *what is* he was rather than the *what if* he wanted them to believe he was, he was able to help them all reach their full potential and even realize their dreams and see that the power, the answers, and the peace of mind they had spent their entire lives seeking from other people had really been inside them all along. Is it possible that our anxiety has things to teach us too?

Much like the Tin Man got a heart-shaped watch, the Scarecrow a diploma, and the Lion a medal of valor in *The Wizard of Oz*, I left therapy with new tools in my tool kit to help me manage my anxiety. Tools I want to now pass along to you because I'm all about sharing practical tips to help people pump the brakes on panic:

1. Staying mindful. It sounds so simple in theory, but getting out of the *what if* of our heads and back into the *what is* of our lives can sometimes feel like a game of tug-of-war. One of my favorite exercises for bringing myself back to the present moment is the Five Senses Game. It's so easy. You pause, take a look at your surroundings, and name five things you can see, four things you can touch, three things you can hear, two things you can smell, and one thing you can

taste. This very simple process has a way of grounding you back into the present and getting you out of your head, where those racing and anxious thoughts occur. Also, a trick I learned more recently: If you find yourself on the verge of a panic attack, shocking your system by splashing really cold water on your face or sniffing something pungent like an alcohol pad will sometimes pull you out of your *what if* mentality and back into your *what is* reality.

2. Breathing / progressive muscle relaxation. Take a few moments and focus on your breathing. Place one hand on your belly and take deep breaths from your diaphragm, making an effort to push your hand out when you inhale. After a few deep, cleansing breaths, try some progressive muscle relaxation. You can google this and find very specific instructions on how to do it, but the essence of progressive muscle relaxation is to focus on tensing up and then relaxing various muscle groups. I always start at my feet and work my way up to my head. It takes only about five minutes, but by the time I'm done, I can feel the tension literally melting from my body. Out of my entire anxiety tool kit, I think this one might be most helpful to me.

3. Social media detox. Take a few days or a weekend and completely unplug from your phone, social media, and/or the outside world. People are like computers: Sometimes we just need to breathe and reboot. Hitting the pause button on the constant stream of breaking news and urgent text messages

and Facebook updates will do wonders for your soul. Spend that time focusing on the people right in front of you rather than the ones in your phone. After a few hours, you probably won't miss your virtual world at all.

4. Self-care Saturday or Sunday. One of my favorite ways to practice self-care is to take one day out of the weekend and do nothing but exactly what I want to do. Read a good book. Watch movies in your pj's all day. Take a walk and get some fresh air. There is nothing more healing and restorative than spending time in nature. Take a hot bubble bath and do a hydrating face mask. Do things that feed your soul, even if what feeds your soul is doing nothing at all. I think you'll find that sometimes doing nothing is absolutely *everything*.

5. Meditation. Guided meditation is one of my favorite ways not just to relax but to fall asleep. Often, anxiety can wreak havoc on our sleep cycle. There's a free app called Insight Timer that has literally thousands of free guided meditations on any and every topic you can imagine. I'm also a huge fan of the Calm app, which isn't free but is well worth the investment. Meditations range from five minutes to an hour and beyond, so whether you do a quick one in the morning to start your day or a long one at night to unwind, there's a meditation for every purpose, topic, and schedule.

These five tips have all been hugely beneficial to me on my path to healing and wholeness. Pick the one or ones that you think will work for you, and feel free to branch out and try other methods to add to this list as well.

My anxiety has been an ever-present shadow in my life, sometimes protecting me from something my mind wasn't yet ready to process, sometimes helping me by pushing me to succeed, and sometimes hurting me by leaving me panic-stricken and wrung out. I might never need intensive therapy for my anxiety again, or I might need it again next week or next month or next year. I've made peace with that. I hope that if you are someone who also lives with anxiety as a constant companion, you'll learn to make peace with it too. The important thing to remember is that there is no one way to overcome anxiety, nor is there one right way. Nor is there any guarantee that you'll ever completely overcome it at all. Everyone's path is different, and that's okay. At the end of the day, what matters is remembering that whatever comes your way, you really *are* enough to handle it, anxiety and all. And though you might never completely get rid of it, you *can* learn to manage your anxiety instead of letting it manage you. It just might take you a few tries to get there. And that's okay.

15

What If I'm Not Enough?

I couldn't write a book about stepping out of the shadows and turning toward the sun, about letting go of the *what if* and embracing the *what is*, without talking about one of the biggest *what ifs* that women wrestle with in the deepest recesses of our hearts (especially single women): *What if I'm not enough?*

This might come as a surprise to some people, but I have gone through much of my life feeling somewhat invisible, even lacking. It might sound strange since I am seemingly a highly visible and even successful person on the career front. But I seem to be someone who gets brushed aside and forgotten by people quite often: friends, romantic prospects and boyfriends, publishers, other fellow writers, even the church itself. A recurring theme of my life seems to be that I attract people who don't always see my value or my worth. This has been especially frustrating for me as I've gotten older and have finally learned to see it for myself. I have the word *enough* tattooed on my wrist; I've even written a book titled *You Are Enough*, and still . . . at times . . . I ask myself, *What if I'm not enough?*

Way back when I first started my career, I was a television producer. I spent a year hustling as an associate producer for the local ABC affiliate in Nashville before landing my dream job at Country Music Television, or CMT.

When I arrived at CMT, fresh off the heels of heartbreak caused by my exodus from the church body I had been a part of for five years that had left me constantly questioning my worth, I was feeling wounded but free. I was ready to embrace my new job and my new life with open arms. I felt like surely I had found "my people." Fellow creatives. People who were as passionate about entertainment news and music and pop culture as I was. I knew I would be welcomed and appreciated for exactly who I was.

But I wasn't. Don't get me wrong; my job was a joy. Ninety-nine percent of the people I worked with during that time were a joy. But a few others were older, somewhat cynical types who I felt were constantly nitpicking my actions. Granted, I was twenty-four and clueless about life, and I know without a doubt that at times I acted twenty-four and clueless about life. But I was also enthusiastic and energetic and darn good at my job. And yet, despite my work performance, I heard comments about my clothes or my shoes or my friendships with the guys at work: I wore heels too often. I dressed too cute. I was friends with too many guys at work (I had both male and female friends—not that it should really matter). Once again, as I had at the church I had broken free from, I felt like I was too much and yet not enough. And, once again, my "not quite fitting in" caused me to lose things dear and precious to me . . . ultimately, both my job and my self-confidence. For those of you keeping score, I had now had my heart broken by both the Christian world and the secular world. I didn't feel like I was enough for either one. And I was left floundering.

After a year or so, I started on a new career path in public relations, one I would stay on until I transitioned to full-time writing.

Strangely enough, the phenomenon of feeling unseen led me to start writing professionally in the first place. The year was 2009. I had just broken free from an unhealthy relationship, and though it was a break that needed to happen, it left me feeling lost and bereft and unsure of where to go next. I was single for the first time in a year and a half and desperately trying to reconnect with the parts of myself I had lost during the relationship: my creative side, my positive, hopeful side, my sassy side.

That led me to start writing. Writing had always been a great love of my life, and putting words to paper seemed to serve as something of a road map for me. I would find myself again in the writing. I would find clarity. I would find meaning. Writing has allowed me to view the big picture of my life in a way that nothing else can. In the writing, I make peace with the *what if*s and embrace the *what is*. In the writing, I find my way back to the sun. In the writing, I feel wonderfully, beautifully *seen* and *enough*.

I didn't see anyone else writing about singleness in a positive way, so I decided that would be the mantle I would take up. I would write about my single journey in a real, honest, and humorous way (because let's face it—single life is nothing if not funny). I would share my stories and the lessons I had learned along the way of being single and thirtysomething. I would give a voice to single women everywhere. I was excited about the idea of this new adventure and where it might take me. Never in my wildest dreams did I dare to imagine it would take me everywhere that it has, to you now holding my sixth book in your hands. With that one (seemingly small at the time) decision to start a blog, I changed my life forever. I changed my career forever. I changed *me* forever. And hopefully something I've said along the way has helped change some of you forever.

In the midst of my own struggles with often feeling unseen and insignificant . . . I was able to give a voice to single women around the world who had also felt unseen and insignificant for far too long. I also began to find my own voice. And I found myself again, reflected back to me in the faces of women around the world who connected with my words. It turned out my story was *their* story. We were all The Single Woman.

And over the years, my beautiful readers, you have helped me find myself time and time again. You have helped me be brave enough to share my stories and my fears and my wins and my losses and my wounds. You have given me a safe, welcoming space to just be Mandy and to feel like that is enough. You have loved and accepted and *seen* me. And I hope I have given some of those gifts back to you.

The flip side of being a professional writer, however, is that, inevitably, you draw not just fans and supporters but onlookers. And those onlookers, for some reason, expect you to be superhuman. I'm not sure why that is. Perhaps it's the nature of what I write about—life, and trying to make sense of it—that leads people to believe that I either have it all figured out or should have it all figured out. But that's kind of the point of me being a writer in the first place— the fact that I don't have anything figured out—and I write through it all to try to piece together this great big, confusing puzzle we call life.

And over the course of the past ten years of writing my way through life, some of these onlookers have muttered under their breath, subtweeted or texted in my direction, or just outright stated that because I make mistakes, get angry and say things in the heat of the moment when I'm hurt or vulnerable, fall for wrong people, and make bad life decisions—because I happen to be human—the things I write about are somehow not real or authentic or heart-felt or true. And if that's the way it works, then I guess paintings and songs and books and movies and all other works of art are also not real or true or legit or authentic. Because behind every creative endeavor is a very flawed, and very human, *human*. So, once again, even as I fight to give a voice to the unseen, I often find myself in a position of feeling like I'm not enough and like I'm being seen not for who I truly am—but for who people expect me to be. Someone who's perfect and succinct and has it all together. And I am none of those things. I am just someone who happens to write words for a living. And those words may not always be the right words or the perfect words, but I think it's pretty brave to throw something creative, something inspired by your own life, out there into the universe and let it land however it lands. I also think it's really cowardly to sit on the sidelines and criticize those of us who are out here on the front lines living our lives in a public manner in hopes that sharing the ashes of our own lives will help others tap into their inner phoenix.

It's a never-ending battle to be myself and to be content that being myself is *enough* . . . and I think it's a battle that most women are facing right along with me. We're not supposed to be content with ourselves and celebrate who we are, because that makes us "too arrogant." But then when we're left questioning ourselves and our worth based on some label society or our boss or even a holier-than-thou stranger has given us, we're dubbed "too insecure."

Too much and never enough.

This isn't a cry for help or a pity party. It's just a recognition of something that has caused me a lot of pain on my journey, and perhaps it's a lifeline for anyone out there who also feels this way and wrestles with the many *what if*s. Just know you're not alone. You're *not* invisible. You *do* matter. You *are* valuable. You *are* enough. You *are* seen. I see you. I've made it my life's work to see you. And I suppose if this lifelong feeling of invisibility has helped inspire my quest to make other women feel seen in this world . . . it's worth it to me.

God says in Isaiah, "I'd never forget you—never" (49:15). So during those moments when we feel unseen and unloved and undervalued and inadequate, we can cling to that truth and carry on. And we can be most assured that even when it feels like we are invisible to the entire world, the God of the universe sees and loves and pursues us. Maybe we can just dwell in the unseen and allow it to be a place of respite and peace rather than uncertainty and unrest. Maybe, just maybe, we can start to see emptiness as openness and room to bloom. And maybe we can trust that when the time is right, Jesus will pluck us out of obscurity and open the eyes of everyone around us. But until then, He wants to keep us to Himself. And when you look at it that way . . . "unseen" suddenly starts to feel like a very beautiful thing, indeed.

One day several years ago, while pondering my enoughness, I came across this Scripture, and though I was sure I had read it a million times before, it reached out and grabbed my heart in a new way:

> Taking her hand, [Jesus] said to her . . . "Young woman, get up." (Mark 5:41 CEB)

It made me cry in the best way. I love Jesus and His heartbeat for women. Especially women the world has forgotten about, tossed aside, or kicked down in the dirt. Women who feel unseen. Women who struggle to believe that they are enough.

Jesus sees us. He redeems us. He qualifies us when others disqualify us. He forced others to see and redeem and qualify the women of the New Testament, and it was completely scandalous for His time and such a thing of beauty.

I don't put a lot of faith in the machine of "Christianity" these days, but I will always put my faith in Jesus . . . because He puts His faith in me.

And in you. Whatever floor or hopeless place or rock bottom you've found yourself in tonight, look up. He's there to meet you, right there in the middle of the unseen, and take your hand and say, "Young woman, get up."

Not long after reading that Scripture, I knew it was time to finally let go of the *what ifs* of my long-ago failed television career and step into the *what is* of who I was now. It was time for me to get up.

So I put on the boldest red dress I could find, and for the first time since I had been let go from my dream job all those years ago, I went to the CMT Awards with my head, heels, and confidence high. Because the people who crushed my TV career in the palm of their hands all those years ago didn't crush me. I had gone on to do exactly what God had called me to do. I had gotten up and gotten on with it, I had stood and I had dealt, I had turned toward the sun, and in the process, I had grown into someone who made other women feel seen, just by being me. Nothing more, nothing less. So much, and perfectly enough.

So now I encourage you to just be *you*, regardless of who has a problem with it. You can't get to your destination in someone else's lane. And you certainly can't get there by constantly stopping to apologize for who you are. Being yourself is the hardest and scariest and best thing you will ever do. It won't always be enough for everyone. There will be lonely times. Seasons of solitude and uncertainty and disappointment. And falls and fails and tears and heart-breaks and dead-end roads and crazy bosses and stupid boys (in the words of Keith Urban, which feels fitting here) and dreams delayed and even denied all together, but there will also be joy and magic and the unwavering confidence of knowing you didn't sacrifice parts of yourself to fit someone else's mold.

Young woman, get up. Be who you are. Messy and imper-fect and flawed as that may be. Because you might be all of those things . . . but you're also **bold** and *italic* and never, ever generic, and it is oh so unique and so perfectly enough.

As for me? I'll keep on writing. And I'll keep on living my imperfect life and trying to make sense of it through my writing, hopefully inspiring a few people along the way to live their own *what if* and *what is* a little more bravely and hopefully making people like me, and maybe even those not like me, feel *seen*. I may not have all the answers, but I'll definitely never stop asking the questions. And I won't ever again apologize for any part of me, the sassy or the spiritual, the anxious or the brave, the me that doubts or the me that has faith. Because all those things make me *me* and make me human . . . and it's my humanness that allows people to relate to my writing (and any good writing, for that matter). Being a human is hard and heartbreaking at times, but I won't let fear stop me, I won't let anyone else's inability to see my worth stop me, and I certainly won't let *what if* stop me.

Don't let it stop you from being whatever and whoever you want to be either.

EPILOGUE

As I write this, I'm sitting in my apartment surrounded by boxes. Am I coming or going, you ask? I'm not sure yet. I'll let you know when I decide.

I'm also surrounded by unknowns and *what if*s. Nothing is certain, and nothing is decided. My parents and I live in the in-between every day with their health. They're not where they were a few months ago. But they're not yet where I'd like them to be either. We have no guarantees at this point what next year or next month or even next week will look like. But still . . . we carry on. We turn toward the sun. We surrender control. And we live in this moment, trusting that the next one and the next one and the next one will take care of themselves. That's all we can do, really. I could let every day overwhelm me with its many *what if*s, but I choose to live in the *what is*. And the *what is* might hold uncertainty, but it also holds joy. It holds peace. It holds me, and it holds my parents, firmly in its grasp. All we have right now is the here and now. And for now, it is enough.

My career is one great big *what if*. With every book I write, there's always the possibility that it might be the last. Writing tends to be either feast or famine. You're always kind of living on a wing and a prayer that people will keep showing up and reading your work. I've thought about getting my master's degree and pursuing a more secure career path, complete with a 401(k) and a retirement plan, but I haven't yet settled on which direction I want to go. That used to scare me. Now it excites me. Because even *if* I never write another book, I'll still have a story to tell. And, ultimately, it will be one of victory and not defeat, of healing and not hurt, of turning away from the shadows and back toward the sun . . . no matter what life throws at me.

My love life is definitely filled with *what if*s. *What if I never find anyone? What if I end up alone? What if I never have a family of my own?* I'm not officially dating again. I'm just starting to take my first hesitant steps in that direction. Although I like to think I'll find someone and that together we'll write a beautiful love story, as of right now, that story is "To Be Continued . . ." But when the *what if*s start to creep up on me and make me question everything about myself, I plant myself firmly in the *what is*. And *what is* is that I know I'll be fine, whichever way it goes. If it turns out that I am a sunflower meant to stand tall and proud and free and alone . . . I will still choose to keep turning toward the sun and living my life to the last drop. And on days when I can't find the sun, I'll turn toward my family and my friends and my faith and myself for warmth. Because the most definitive *what is* in my life is that I know I can count on myself. How do I know this? I survived a pandemic alone. I stood by my parents and we gazed directly into the eye of cancer, and I didn't flinch or back down. And I might have bent, but I never broke. I look back now at that frantic, anxious version of 2020 me with so much love. She *survived*. And eventually . . . she *thrived*. And you will too, whatever *what if* you might be facing today. You just have to live your way to it.

I remember days, not too long ago, when I didn't laugh for a long time. When life felt heavy and sad and overwhelming. When I would turn away from the sun rather than toward it like the sunflowers do. There is one day that stands out, back in December 2020, when nothing in my life had felt happy for a really, really long time. And then one day, it snowed, which isn't all that typical for Tennessee, even in the winter. I took a walk down Main Street, where I live, and for once, all was calm and all was bright. And as I was standing out in the peaceful quiet of the snow, watching it swirl around me like I was inside a snow globe, tears of joy began to fall down my face and mix with the snowflakes. And in that moment, I felt God whisper, "I did this just for you." And in that moment, I realized: This is the beauty, and the magic, of the *what is*. Yes, you will know struggle. But you will also know the simple pleasures of *just being alive*.

Nowadays, I am always on the lookout for finding joy in the ordinary and opportunities to turn toward the sun: Mom eating really well or having a good day. The church bells chiming on Sunday mornings. A drive out into the country. A hug from my dad. The lemony smell of the magnolia trees hanging thick in the air on a hot summer's day. A good book. A funny meme. My cat, warm and snuggly, purring next to me. Laughing with my sister. A text from an old friend. The beautiful, ordinary magic of the *what is*. And I'm grateful . . . so grateful that I hung on through the gray days as flat as the Kansas prairie and made it back to the Emerald City of color and light. And along the way, I made friends and I lost friends and I often felt scared and powerless and alone. But at the end of the yellow brick road, I realized that no matter how lost I might get, the power to come home to myself had been mine all along. And I click my ruby-red sandals together and laugh, because where there is laughter, there is healing. And year forty-two for me has been all about healing. And choosing, every day, to surrender control and live in this moment instead of worrying about all the ones still to come. And turning toward the sun.

I hope wherever you are in your journey, in the midst of the gray days or the sunny days, you remember that always, always hovering just above even the darkest, most ominous clouds is the sun. And one day soon, it will shine again. And one day soon, you will laugh again. And one day soon, life will be warm and bright and happy again. As long as you keep reaching, keep hoping, keep letting go of the *what if*, keep embracing the *what is*, and keep turning toward the sun . . . eventually you'll find it. And you'll once again bask in its glow.

And in your own.

The End.

ACKNOWLEDGMENTS

I would like to thank everyone at Revell and Baker Publishing Group, especially Vicki Crumpton and Michele Misiak, not just for helping me bring this book to life but for your immense grace and patience and understanding as I took time away from my writing to take care of my family. You were truly the hands and feet of Jesus.

To my agent, Alex Field: THANK YOU for always having my back and for making sure nothing writing-related got lost in the shuffle when my world fell apart. I am eternally grateful.

To my dear friend Laura: Thank you for your unconditional love and support and prayers and for truly being my most faithful friend.

To Michael: Thank you for always answering my middle-of-the-night phone calls, even all these years later.

To Jaclyn King and the entire staff of Christian Life Church: Thank you for your fervent prayers. They truly held us up in those early days. My family and I love you and are so thankful for you.

To my cousins Jason, Melanie, and Emma and my uncle Vernie and aunt Wardene: Your generosity knows no bounds. We love you so much.

To my surrogate "aunts," Marcia and Barbara: The way you have loved on my family and stood with us means more than you will ever know. I love you both dearly.

To everyone who called, texted, prayed, sent a meal or a gift card, and just generally loved us through the most challenging and heartbreaking season of our lives: A million thank-yous would never be enough. But here's one anyway: THANK YOU. Your kindness and love literally carried us through.

And finally, to Mom, Dad, Cher, Kevin, Emma, and Livi: Thank you for being "my people." Not my perfect Hallmark-movie people but my wild, loud, imperfect National Lampoon people. We are just the right mix of chaos and love. And we will not EVER be defeated.

NOTES

Chapter 7 What If He's the One?

1. Wikipedia, s.v. "Negging," last modified October 6, 2021, 18:53, http://en.wikipedia.org/wiki/Negging.
2. Toni Morrison, *Jazz* (New York: Penguin, 2007), 135.
3. Mandy Hale, *Don't Believe the Swipe: Finding Love without Losing Yourself* (Grand Rapids: Revell, 2021), 18.

Chapter 8 How to Let Go of Love

1. *Titanic*, directed by James Cameron (Hollywood, CA: Paramount Pictures, 1997).
2. Elizabeth Gilbert, *Eat, Pray, Love: One Woman's Search for Everything Across Italy, India, and Indonesia* (New York: Penguin, 2007), 164.
3. *Sex and the City*, season 2, episode 1, "Take Me Out to the Ball Game," directed by Allen Coulter, written by Darren Star, Michael Patrick King, and Candace Bushnell, aired June 6, 1999, on HBO

Chapter 10 Turning Toward the Son

1. Laura Robinson (@LauraRbnsn), Twitter, June 6, 2021, https://twitter.com/laurarbnsn/status/1401545958534619136?lang=fa.

Chapter 13 Decoding Mysterious Male Behavior

1. Hale, *Don't Believe the Swipe*, 90.

Chapter 14 Anxiety

1. Mandy Hale, *You Are Enough: Heartbreak, Healing, and Becoming Whole* (New York: Hachette, 2018).

Mandy Hale is a blogger turned *New York Times* bestselling author and speaker. Creator of the social media movement The Single Woman, Mandy cuts to the heart of single life with her inspirational, straight-talking, witty takes on life and love. Named a "Twitter Powerhouse" by the *Huffington Post*, a "Woman of Influence" by the *Nashville Business Journal*, one of the "10 Instagram Accounts to Follow for Major Inspiration" by *Good Morning America*, and a "Single in the City" by *Nashville Lifestyles* magazine, she has also been featured in *USA Today* and *Forbes* magazine, on Glamour.com, and in many other media outlets. She is the author of several books, including *Don't Believe the Swipe*. She lives in Murfreesboro, Tennessee. Learn more at www.mandyhale.com.